- A challenge that life accepts

Raghavendra Pati Tripathi
Parul Tripathi

First Published in January 2022

ISBN: 978-93-5472-953-9

BLUEROSE PUBLISHERS

www.bluerosepublishers.com

info@bluerosepublishers.com

+91 8882 898 898

Cover Design:

Aveek

Typographic Design:

Rohit

Distributed by: BlueRose, Amazon, Flipkart

We dedicate this book

to

our Readers & Well-wishers!

ARE YOU READY TO ACCEPT THE CHALLENGE...???

When I embarked on my journey to bring about a radical transformation among the people through 'Fear can be overcome', my concern was to approach it in a humanitarian way so that it may facilitate and help everyone during their dire needs. As we all know, the horizon of fear is very vast and everyone comes in its grip sooner or later and goes through unlimited trauma.

I have shared my own life experiences as it has provided me a chance to see the real world of fear which might look fascinating for a new generation. I have been very curious since my childhood and whenever fear gripped me in its clutches, I tried to understand whether it's me who was scared or people with whom I was familiar with fear or a majority of people fear or was it everyone? The curiosity kept growing with each passing day.

I started to search for the causes of fear. In this regard, I often used to ask the elderly people, "Do you fear?" Generally, they used to smile or laugh or sometimes be astonished at my question. Some of them very affectionately used to ask me, "Son, what do you want to know? Just study and play, you will get your desired answer at the right time." I was never satisfied and my efforts to find the answers went on and on. Gradually I began to realize why people fear. And finally, the time has arrived to reveal it, that's why- I am before you.

This book revolves around how to overcome fear and especially fear of failure as it's the most terrible fear which also consists of criticism and fear of social rejection. The increasing pressure from all corners of the society hampers an individual's performance and he is destined to live in the realm of fear.

Unconditional love and acceptance are the hallmark to connect each individual with the mainstream and enable them to understand that they are very precious for society. This will boost up their confidence and they will be able to empower themselves as well as the society and the nation. They will be eager to try their best to prove their worth as per their ability and potential. Our main focus consists in bringing out the enormous potentials of each individual and integrating it with a positive attitude for their well-being.

It is vital to know that you are an unique individual. Momentary achievements make no difference at all. So, just be happy. If you are having a positive attitude towards life then you will be able to face the problems easily. So, release your tension and relax in your own world. No need to get irritated in any situation, just do your best. Be gentle with yourself but determined enough to achieve your goal. Give yourself sufficient space to grow but remember that outcome depends on God's will not yours.

Our life is a blessing of God. Always believe in your

uniqueness and believe in your ability. Whatever you have been deprived of once in your life in a numerical way, you will be able to get back all the compensation in multiple ways. Destiny plays a key role in your life and throws many challenges to test your ability and potential. Testing time comes to prove your worth so focus on facing the challenges instead of raising doubts on yourself. Never underestimate your merit and ability to recover from failure. As we know that the ability to fail big and fail often has been a mark of the spectacularly successful people throughout history, so, always think that you are quite capable of turning the wheel of fortune in your favour and it is for granted that you can overcome fear. I am a firm believer in the existence of God. He is always with me and obliges whenever I need Him. Each time my faith increases and I express my devotion to Him.

My daughter Parul Tripathi, co-author of this book has been a source of inspiration throughout this journey and her valuable suggestions have been the core components in the successful completion of the book. Her insights combined with her precious experiences which she came across while studying and working in various parts of the globe have truly been helpful. Her understanding of human behaviour from the perspective of a human being and a psychologist has been the hallmark of this book.

The words fail to express my gratitude for my younger daughter Himanshi Tripathi who has been my lifeline throughout this period with her immense support. Her positive feedback encouraged and boosted up my confidence to put extra effort on my part. She deserves a lot of credit due to her enormous contribution. This book could not be completed without the loving and caring support of my wife Shashi Tripathi whom I appreciate and admire wholeheartedly.

I am immensely thankful to all my beloved ones.I would be pleased if this book will facilitate in enlightening someone.I am grateful to all my readers and eagerly awaiting your responses.

Raghavendra Pati Tripathi

FACE TO FACE.....!!

There comes a time in everyone's lives where we are at a place that can be probably deemed as our lowest. Shattered, exhausted, unclear of the next plan of action and simply scared of what lies ahead. But in the deepest of our vulnerabilities, lies the greatest of our capabilities. Our strength and resilience are there somewhere lying dormant amidst the clouds of fear, self-doubt and hopelessness. Our fears cloud our judgment, ability to think what we are truly capable of. Once we are out of it, the magic starts unfolding. There's no rocket science behind it, just a mere orchestration of your own minds. You believe what it makes you believe, you think what it makes you think and ultimately you become what you believe.

So, the key to this juggle is simple- "your mind" and how you mould it and tame it to make sure it isn't stronger than thou is what will set you apart. This book aims to inspire each one of you who has been through or going through a dark phase and struggling to find a way out. I have managed to escape from the dark hole that kept pulling me back, gathered my strength and re-incarnated a better and stronger self. With this book, I hope you do too!

The time we all are living in is more uncertain than ever. The ongoing Covid crisis and other major challenges going around in the world has turned all our lives upside down in some way or the other. We fell short of resources, devoid from meeting our loved ones, dubious about our jobs still being intact- fear seemed to dominate every aspect of our lives. We are still in some capacity recovering from the trauma and fear we have gone through. The fear of losing something is paramount and when it involves ourselves and our loved ones, it is even scarier. While I saw my world turning around, witnessing incessant cries for help, watching loved ones fall sick, losing them- it all seemed like a dreaded nightmare. All I wondered was if I'll ever be able to recover from the shadow of these dark times. But I did. . . . I vowed to myself that I am not going to let the past deter my present or future. This made me think about what I can do to make sure that I can reach out to as many people as possible who have gone through a similar circumstance at some point in their lives. The truth is we all have been there. The only difference is, some of us have skillfully managed to escape the shadows of our pre-existing fear, for some of us it is an ongoing battle of fighting our inner demons and the rest probably haven't gathered the courage to begin yet. So, to all of you who are reading this book, I want to assure you that you are capable, you are worthy and you are certainly "bigger than your fears".

I would like to extend my heartiest gratitude to my father for giving me this opportunity to contribute to this book. He has always been my biggest supporter and stood by me like a rock in every walk of my life. A major shout out to my mother, Shashi Tripathi and sister, Himanshi Tripathi for being a perpetual source of inspiration and being my emotional guide. Gran Mags, Margaret Miller, whose constant love and care have kept me going even through my darkest times. I would also like to thank all my friends & dear ones for always being there for me, believing in me and for their constant encouragement. Last but not the least, a round of appreciation to all my well-wishers, who despite not knowing me on a personal level have always wished the best for me. I see you and value you. Thank you to each one of you for inspiring me to be a better version of myself every single day.

I hope that "Fear can be overcome" gives the reader the perspective they are searching for, the ability to introspect and the courage to realize their true potential.

"It is only in our darkest hours, we see the light, it is only at our lowest we discover how high we can fly."

Parul Tripathi

FEAR CAN BE OVERCOME – A CHALLENGE THAT LIFE ACCEPTS

CONTENTS

1. Peeping Into The Fascinating World Of Fear......... 1
2. Does Fear Really Exist? A Substantial Issue. 18
3. Fear As It Propagates- An Interaction With Reality.. 36
4. Is Fear Universal?- Horizon Of Fear 52
5. Fear- A Disease Or A Conceptual State Of Mind 66
6. The Fingerprints Of Fear- An analytical Approach 79
7. Channelization Of Fear:- The Need Of Hour 91
8. Believe In Yourself - Explore your potential 105
9. Fear Can Be Overcome- A Challenge That Life Accepts 119

PEEPING INTO THE FASCINATING WORLD OF FEAR

" Life is never easy, we have to make it easy, sometimes by ignoring something and sometimes by accepting something."

The concept of fear has originated since the rise of human civilization and its impact on human beings has been enormous. With the arrival of a new version of fear- 'COVID-19', fear has been incorporated in our day to day lives and we are compelled to live with it. In every walk of life its presence can be felt easily but the question is... "Were we never accustomed to face fear before COVID-19 in such a critical way?" The answer is that life can't be imagined without the concept of fear and as a human we have to accept it, face it and find a way to overcome it. So, exploring the various facets of fear in order to be able to face them and deal with them courageously is the ardent need of the hour.

Whenever I see scary faces, I always try to connect a relation among them which are the root causes for occurring fear but most of the time I end up finding a new reason which creates fear. The horizon of fear is so vast and full of uncertainties which makes it fascinating because sometimes a pleasing moment of someone's life suddenly turns into a bitter experience of life and the scars of fear are difficult to heal. It is a never ending process of our whole life which everyone is bound to face- willingly or unwillingly. Willingly means sometimes we get involved in many actions and activities fully aware of how difficult it is and are ready to face the heat and unwillingly means we are forced to accept it as a part and parcel of life. And, in this process life just goes on.

It might look strange to someone with due honour to his own thinking but my perception leads me to the conclusion that life is the second eternal reality of this world after the evolution of the Universe. I did not mention God here as He is the creator of both. Each moment of life is a reality which cannot be ignored and some of these moments of life become milestones and make life more beautiful and more meaningful. Human life is said to be the most precious gift of God on the earth which provides a chance to see this strange world and create a unique identity for oneself by overcoming all the fear that comes in our way.

I don't want to roam into the world of imagination to bring out a hypothetical interesting story to preach to someone. I also don't mean to say that such things are not useful for us in any way. Motivation in any form is a healing process which helps people in their dire needs. But, at this time, I am peeping into the real world of fear and in this regard, first and foremost trying to look back into my past. The experience of my own life has provided me a clear vision to see and analyze the various facets of fear. It is a fact that anyone can forget the happiest moment of his life though temporarily but never forgets the one which he has encountered in the realm of fear.

Those memories always exist and I am recalling my own experiences which are lying dormant in my heart and are bubbling to come out.

I consider myself a child of destiny as the journey of my life has been a true testimony of fluctuating fortunes. I have been a witness to such ordinary and extraordinary happenings throughout the course of time that have propelled me to pen down the experiences which might be useful for laymen in the terrible situations when someone is surrounded by fear. Reasons may be different but the trauma they face is more or less similar. Starting from the day when as a child, anyhow I was able to understand the happenings of our day-to-day life to the present, I always wonder that in spite of their enormous talent, power and financial status, people tend to live in the shadow of fear. It has become an unavoidable companion and everyone is bound to live with this illusion.

I grew up in a remote village where there was no sign of good basic facilities such as good educational institutes, proper connectivity from the city, and the list was so long. But, people did not care much for such facilities as they were devoted to their respective works in earning basic requirements to move on. A sense of satisfaction was everywhere. Life was very simple and people used to enjoy each moment of life but it doesn't mean that they were free from the clutches of fear. Actually, the presence of fear was more than that of at present. They were so habitual of living together that they lacked self-confidence especially when they had to face the process of life alone. The feeling of insecurity to encounter the challenge used to instill fear.

The reason might be different for each individual but fear exists. It's true that when we are continuously caught in the same situations, slowly and slowly we become able to overcome our fear.

Darkness was one of the prime factors of fear in those days. A myth had crept in people's minds that ghosts and witches rule during nights. Though scientists laugh at this concept, it can be seen even today that a majority of people believe in this notion. We were so terrified that whenever we used to go outside of our home due to important work, this thought always remained in our mind that we had to return before the sunset. Some places were identified where there were more possibilities of ghosts and witches. Though it might look humorous to us today that particular places were ruled by ghosts and witches while travelling at night while in the daytime it looked quite normal.

The above incidences of fear which I have mentioned here may be categorized as a common fear which everybody has to go through during their lifespan but gradually they realize the cause behind it and thus are able to handle it properly and no harm is done. Later on in our life we share it with our young generation and laugh. Such incidents are a source of amusement for the current generation as today's children are much smarter and also well equipped and they don't believe in myths easily. During childhood, I used to think that it was only the children who fear but later, I witnessed a totally different scenario. I find that the horizon of fear develops as a never ending phenomenon and we are bound to live in it.

A remarkable fact which makes fear strange is that people are more cautious and anxious, less for themselves and more for their families. Actually, the problem is that parents want to dictate the life of their wards and in this process, they end up mounting a huge amount of pressure not only on themselves but also on their children and most of the time it hampers the performance of the children. As we all know that each individual is a unique creation of God and is blessed with some vital capabilities which help him to live life happily and flourish as per his or her ability. During my school life, I found that teachers used to give utmost importance to academics. It was assumed that a child good in academics is a guarantee to success. Children were not allowed to spend enough time in sports. Because of this perception, a child hardly got sports facilities and their enormous aptitude was buried due to lack of awareness. We can't blame parents because they followed a set pattern and tried to do what was the most suitable for their wards as per their view point and experience.

A mystery which I often found amusing from my childhood days to present is that a majority of students who didn't perform up to the mark as per the norms of family and society were not bothered about their performance and looked very satisfied with whatever they have achieved. Their main concern was to report about their performances to their parents. They were afraid of being humiliated by their respective parents though it might be their illusion in some cases but it cannot be denied entirely. During school days, some of my classmates were teacher's wards and a couple of them were close friends. Though their parents were ultra protective and were always ready to support them, they didn't want to spend time with their parents. In fact, they were afraid of facing their father as they used to feel suffocated because of their stereotype non-stop preaching which they found very irritating. They used to respect their fathers so much and were unable to protest but it created a distance between them and they were unable to open in terms of likings and dislikings. Their communication was one way. This set up of theory still exists.

It is a common principle that the person whom we love cannot see him get into trouble at any cost. This can be seen everywhere that a person can easily bear the ill- fate of his life but it gives him immense pain when he finds any of his dear ones suffering from the cruel hands of misfortune. It is a true fact that as a human being, we cannot change the situations at our will all the time. We have to accept whatever comes in our way as a result of previous life's deeds (karma) and it is not only for a few people but for all. Actually people are not ready to accept it. Though majority of people believe in destiny but they try to change it or overpower it as per their desires. Future is unseen but we tend to unfold it always and in the process doubts come. When such a thought comes to the mind that is fluctuating between positives and negatives then no one can focus. I want to mention our culture here, as it is a boon for us. It teaches us the importance of sacrifice. In such cases, fear becomes a great purpose for us to fulfill our responsibilities which everyone is deliberately accepting generation by generation and the complaints are yet to be registered in this case.

It has become very common to see the majority of parents waiting anxiously outside the gate of examination centres. The agony and tension can easily be seen on their faces. Even the parents whose wards are proven scholars and are confident to do well yet they don't relax. It is due to examination fear because sometimes brilliant students also aren't able to convert their ability and knowledge into performance. There can be many reasons behind it but the fear of failure is definitely involved. The result of any examination is based on the performance of the students in that specific time period. There are so many limitations in each examination in which certain rules and regulations are involved. Besides norms, there are other factors also which affect the performance of a student such as- health of students, ability to give answers in stipulated time, environment of the examination hall etc. Though these factors look very common, they are very vital in determining the outcome. There are many instances that in spite of very good preparation for a particular examination, a student is unable to get the desired result. These can be seen as hidden reasons because these are not taken seriously at the initial stages but everybody has to face it when one is caught unfortunately in such situations. People tend to fear thinking about the negative incidents which have already taken place and it is a general human tendency that they think such incidents might happen to them and fear automatically occurs.

We always come across in our daily life witnessing people

indulged in debate in small groups on political, social, religious issues, etc. at family gatherings, social functions, in the market, schools, colleges, offices or everywhere and everyone seems to have a deep knowledge and a good orator. The same set of people whenever asked to address on a stage, hesitate to turn up. It's only a handful who agree , though not willingly. The question is why does this happen? Even a brilliant scholar or student tries to escape to speak in front of a huge gathering though he possesses a deep knowledge on the concerned topic which he has to deliver. It means lack of knowledge is not a single reason behind it but there are other reasons too. I discussed this point with many people and the point of view of everyone was more or less the same. But the point which was common for each one is the feeling of discomfort while addressing a large gathering and it can be improved only by repeatedly performing this skill.

We have come a long way and have developed almost in all domains of life. The developmental processes are still going on to improve the lifestyles of people. Highly reputed educational institutions, Skyscrapers, modern transportation facilities, luxurious items for daily life, internet connectivity to monitor and connect with the whole world are some examples of achievements. Every light has its own shadow whose presence cannot be ignored. In spite of so much development and various programmes undertaken by the government to uplift the condition of its citizens, more effort is still required. A large majority of people throughout the world are still in search of earning their next bread for them. Even they fear to see the dream of luxurious life as they are passing their time in the cruel reign of reality. They don't care much for education. The fear of people living in such conditions can be understood but the people who are fortunate enough to enjoy all the required facilities without any problem are living in the shadow of fear much more than the poor ones and it makes fear magical. The main problem is that a person who is living in so- called good or better condition always wants to maintain this and the idea of losing this status instills fear in their mind.

Foeticide is a curse for any society or nation but it is a never ending social stigma. The government and NGOs are doing their best to eradicate this heinous crime but they are unable to fulfill their mission as its roots are so deep. The question is- why are such things happening in society? What is the reason behind it? Such crimes show the mental bankruptcy of an individual as well as society because in such cases both are responsible. This is happening in poor and rich families alike. Sometimes it happens because families lack awareness and they are unable to nourish the child, especially girls. Fostering a child brings fear in their minds and they take up such cruel decisions.

Gender based dissimilarity still exists in our society. Poor, rich, educated, uneducated, men or women, everyone is equally involved in it. Most of the girl children face step motherly behaviour. Some people are so narrow- minded that they want to ensure the gender of their child even before the child is born. If the child is a girl, then a case of foeticide might happen. Such people are mentally ill and they require medical treatment. The fear has grasped their thinking power and they live in the myth that a son takes care of his family and a girl might create problems. They don't know that the time has changed and the girls are flourishing in every field and are acquiring the pole position even in the fields where they were once considered as weak competitors. They are the pride for their parents and are able to change the mindset of society though slowly but their position is far better now.

I have been a part of such a society which always believes that life should be lived as per our ancient culture and it is our moral duty to follow each ritual and tradition without a doubt. Initially I found it interesting and advocated such feelings because I thought such people were keen followers of our culture but later on, I realized that it was my misconception. Actually, what they were doing was totally not their will, it was due to social pressure which often forced them to follow such rituals and traditions. There was fear of being left alone from the social group and they did not have courage to oppose such social pressure. I am mentioning here such incidents which I have witnessed. In our country, certain rituals are performed after the demise of a person for the peace of his soul as it is mentioned in religious books. I am not criticizing such rituals as I have full faith in my culture and traditions. I am just citing whatever a person has to perform under social pressure and which is not mentioned in the religious books. As we know that society is a web of social relationships and we follow the traditions of the society in which we live.

Each society has its own norms which are followed by

everyone without raising a doubt as the norms are set up by the people living in society themselves. With due respect to everyone's feeling, I am sorry to point out that whenever I see the people who are suffering with pain on the demise of their dear ones, sometimes are bound to borrow the money to perform such rituals. The person is rich or poor, employed or unemployed, everybody has to do so. Social pressure counts too much in marriage related matters. Marriage is known as the meeting of two souls. It is a sacred ceremony which was earlier performed in the presence of family gathering with relatives and friends. Nowadays, the scenario has been completely changed. People try to spend beyond their capacity in booking hotels, marriage halls, decorations and arrangements for catering. People do this because of society pressure.

One of the most common fears which I like to gladly face and want to remain in people's mind is fear of God. In this regard, I want to mention a story here which I read during my school days and the reason why I like this fear. This story consists of a father and his son. The father used to tell his son that God is everywhere and he is the witness to all our good and bad deeds. One day they were doing work in their field, and suddenly the father asked his son to keep a watch as he was going to steal from another field. The son agreed. While stealing, every time he asked his son, " Is there anyone watching? Each time his son replied ,"Yes". At last he came out and asked, "who is watching? I am not seeing anyone." The son replied, "God". The father was full of shame and he embraced his son lovingly and affectionately. The story may be real or fictional, it does not matter, only the moral of the story is important.

Later on in my life, I realized that such incidents change the course of life. In our upbringing particularly, we are given such education from our family members. It depends on the family how it is going to instil values in its new generation. The stories of Ramayana, Mahabharata, Puranas, Panchtantra and the pebbles from other religions are a medium of dispersing knowledge in an interesting way and creates an everlasting impact. It is an effort to see things in a right perspective and try to understand what is right and what is wrong. It is emphasized that if anyone does wrong deeds, its outcome which is considered 'sin' will follow him throughout life and he will have to pay the price whatever 'Sin' he has committed.

In the present time, the incidents of violence have become very common and sooner or later everyone has to be a victim- be it physical, mental or emotional trauma. Why are all these things happening? The simple reason- moral values are disappearing. These people don't believe in the supremacy of God when everything is normal but once when they are caught in the hands of misfortune then realize that their wrong deeds are always punished. When a person thinks that he will have to pay for his Karma if not in this life then the next one, this feeling leads him to do good for mankind and thus the fear of God is helpful for human beings.

In this regard, I find it very strange that natural calamities such as earthquakes, tsunami, epidemic, pandemic etc. generate fear when people think about these as these are happening regularly throughout the Globe but people accept it as it is a natural disaster and everyone is affected. It is faced through collective effort. In such cases after destruction, rehabilitation begins and supports come from all corners. Slowly and slowly people forget it as a fearful dream and get involved in their day to day life. I did mention it because the places which are declared as a highly prone area for earthquakes and tsunami are not totally vacant. People are still residing there and are ready to face the fear. It is a deliberate and bold effort to face the fear as they are unable to shift to other places and resettle there.

The fear which I have seen and mentioned earlier generally does not trouble me permanently throughout life. These are for the time being only. People overcome the fear as the time progresses and their doubts regarding the outcome of proceedings becomes clear. The fear in our mind which consists of the well-being and success of our loved ones vanishes when the job is done. As we all know that we are children of destiny, in spite of whatever we do, whatever effort we put in the process of fulfilling our works, our controlling power decides our fate and we are forced to accept it. It is not a matter of our choice. God always does justice and we should never doubt but at the same time we, as a human being, think too much in this regard as it is a general human tendency and when the things are not going as per our wish, we used to blame Him though for a moment.

Particularly in the so- called modern life people believe in the proverb- justice delayed, justice denied. Though It may not be true. In the present time of fierce competition, the bar is so high that we cannot say that we are the victim of injustice whenever we are denied certain opportunities. It happens due to a system in which candidates are selected as per the vacancies and it does not mean that rest are incapable for that particular post. If the efforts are on, one is sure of success but sometimes people are not able to understand the system and need of hour. They consider themselves failures and from here the real problem begins. The fear of failure creeps in their mind. It begins from the school days. We often witness the scene in which a child is pampered by teachers and parents for his excellence particularly in the field of academics. The main point is-nobody wants to go in depth to trace out the reason behind the children who are not performing up to mark and are constantly facing humiliation by teachers and parents. This situation is not limited only for schooling days but it goes on throughout the lifespan of a person. If he is getting the desired result and proving his ability, he is showered with praise and respect. It is very interesting that a child who has been a brilliant student throughout the academics and has been praised for his achievement does not get the same respect in later part of his life if he is unable to convert his academic performance into getting a prestigious job. On the other hand, a child who has been constantly humiliated by his teachers and parents, suddenly with some stroke of luck and most of his will power and hard work is able to earn money, is regarded successful and gets respect.

It is human behaviour that everyone wants a prestigious

place for himself/ herself in the society. When a child grows as an adult, he finds that the people who have achieved success are in the leading position in the society. They are in a role of dictating terms for others. They are enjoying all the benefits and living on their own terms. They are not different from others, the only thing is that they have become successful. It has become a dream of each child to get success. Some people who have not achieved success as per their wish adopt a negative approach as they consider themselves 'failure'. These people always fear that their wards might get the same fate and it leads them towards depression. Some years ago, I read in newspapers that a mother committed suicide when her daughter failed in exam. Such unfortunate incidents happen as they fail to cope up with pressure.

The range of fear of failure is so vast that it encircles each aspect of human life. It does not relate only to score high marks in schools and get a prestigious job. It follows throughout life in each work performed by human beings. The reason which makes it one of the most terrible fears is that it is judged by others, sometimes by those who are not capable of judging others. As it is said- man is a social animal. He is a part of a particular society and cannot live alone. The problem begins from here. It is true that a person is the best judge of himself because he better knows about his/ her strengths and weaknesses and is fully aware of his ability. I have often found that some people who are totally satisfied with their position and are living happily are regarded as failures by society. As we know, God has created us for a particular purpose. The world of work is very vast and each work is equally important for society and nation as these compliment each other.

Nowadays, particularly our children are under tremendous pressure. They are unable to enjoy their life. They are trying their level best in the competitions. They are sacrificing their tender feelings for getting desired success. Whenever I compare the status of the present generation to mine, I find the present one much more dedicated and devoted to their tasks. They are self motivated and want to prove their ability at any cost. In the past, we lacked facilities and awareness. Whatever opportunities came in our way, we accepted and were satisfied. The pressure was minimal.

Now, the situation is different. As much as children are putting hard work, more and more is being expected from them. They have been caught in a dilemma. Fear is like a double edged sword. Have you ever thought, why are people so committed to succeed in spite of so much burden of tension and anxiety? It is happening due to the high level of competition.The past records of achievements are being broken each day and new milestones are being created. It is obvious that when there is pressure, people try their best and put maximum effort. Sometimes it works in their favour and sometimes does not. When the outcome is as per their wish they celebrate and if not, depression follows and from here the problem occurs.

As we know when a seedling is laid, the adventitious branches grow and then the rise of the never terminating giant tree or perhaps in this case the monster. The monster of the present scenario is FEAR. Often, we tend to overlook the cause or the root of fear and take it as a part and parcel of life. It is a great mistake on our part as the problem needs to be sorted out at once through a healing process rather than just going on waiting helplessly. So, now I am starting my voyage in this case and hoping you will join me.

DOES FEAR REALLY EXIST? A SUBSTANTIAL ISSUE.

I have often asked this question since my childhood. I have seen people around me who proclaim to be fearless. You can find such people everywhere- in your family, society, workplace etc. If you try to check the reliability behind their proclaim and enquire in this regard, they seem to be clueless and often you will be amazed to find out that such self- proclaimed fearless people are more fearful than the one who believes in the concept of fear and accepts his fear. The real question here is- Why do people try to run away from reality? We should try to find out these answers and see how they relate to human behaviour.

Probably it involves a valid reason. Maybe such people who proclaim themselves as fearless are merely creating a projection of it and trying to hide their fear . We often tend to forget that the most common way to combat fear is to explore it rather than confining it within ourselves and feeling the suffocation every time we think of it. As much as we are doing so, the intensity of fear increases and it might reach a point from where it could be beyond our reach to handle. So, the first step to overcome fear is ACCEPTANCE.

This situation has yet another side- when the so- called

fearless people interact with the people who are well familiar with their fear and anyhow manage to manipulate about their hidden fear then the vague mist of bogus hypocrisy of the fearless people compels the other category to reflect upon- Does fear really exist? This question leads to a doubt, then a thought and finally emerges out as a full- fledged clear 'misconception' which unfortunately makes them bound to believe the fact that they are probably weaker in terms of handling the terrible situations than those sections of self-proclaimed fearless people. This leads to a degree of inferiority which mounts on to form a heap of insecurity and escapism but it is only momentary, the illusion soon vanishes and from here we believe that one agrees or not, it does not matter. The truth is- fear really exists.

Each individual is a unique creation of God and is blessed with enormous potential to move ahead in life and fulfil his desire. Initially one wants to be fearless but as we know, it is not a choice but it is the reality of life which we cannot deny at any cost. We encounter fear in our day to day life throughout our life span. As a kid, we are unable to understand it but it always exists. We often find in the kids the habit of touching and holding each object they come into contact with. In the process, they become familiar with what is harmful for them and next time they don't touch or hold that object due to fear. They want to protect themselves particularly from fire, darkness, etc.

Family is often considered a heaven on this earth by the people living on this planet but sometimes it is described as hell by few ones or the same people who used to consider it as a paradise but their perception have been changed now. Why does this happen? Such a controversial statement does not come from the positive mind, it comes from the out- burst of feelings which is generated in the heart when someone is caught in the cruel clutches of misfortune. All human beings are living on the same planet so the relation of humanity always exists among them. Though the troubling situation which generates fear and ruins the life might be different but each one is caught in this situation sooner or later. We witness such a family in which when a drunken father enters the house, he creates fear among family members. He makes a lot of noise, abuses and even beats them. He does not care that his wife is tired after the day's work and preparing dinner or his children are preparing for the next day's exam and his act will be harmful for his children. His drunken situation itself shows that he is unable to cope up with the pressure and wants to lose his consciousness in order to get rid of his own fear. How can anyone expect good behaviour from such a person? The burning question is- In such types of cases when a child has to face the fear from his own father, can he easily get over this trauma? The answer is simple- Perhaps No.

Life has different shades. The situations change but the intensity of fear remains the same. We can take up the cases of well organized families whose lifestyle seems like a dream for someone. As much as the position of family is higher in the society, the pressure of delivering good in every field of life is expected higher and higher. The social reputation is always at stake to perform better and maintain a certain level. Family members particularly children and youth are under tremendous pressure to do their best. Their performances are constantly being scanned in comparison to others. Here, there is no physical abuse for getting desired results but the pressure is more. Unconditional love and acceptance is disappearing. Bargaining is going on everywhere. Always there is a condition- If someone is performing as per the desire of their respective parents, he is obtaining each and everything whatever he wants as a token of reward. In case, if unable to perform as per the expected norms- though he is not humiliated physically by his parents but he can easily sense the displeasure of his parents which tells a lot about their inappropriate behavior.

Are we living our normal life as we want? Why don't we get satisfied with whatever we achieve in our life? Is there any prescribed formula to be happy? It is said that the scars of childhood remain forever and it hardly vanishes from our memories. It is a general tendency that whatever we get from our elders, generally the same we disperse it among our children. Should we blame parents for controlling the life of their children as per their wish? Parents dream of a happy and prosperous life for their children much better than theirs in every sphere of life. The assumption that their dear children might not be able to get that position which they are hoping for disturbs them mentally. Looking at the present situation of fierce competition creates doubt first then turns into fear.

Besides family, a child spends most of his time in school before entering into the world of work. School is called the temple of knowledge and is surrounded by a healthy environment which provides each child a chance of overall development and enables them to see things in the right perspective. During my school days, the situation was far more different from today in terms of not only facilities but as per the mind- set of the teachers and students also. At that time, we were afraid of teachers but respect was always there. Nowadays, the students don't fear their teachers and respect...??? But, it doesn't apply to all the students. Corporal punishment was regarded as a blessings of teachers as their integrity was never in question. Neither parents nor students were against it. I did not find anyone objecting to it. We were accustomed to the Gurukul system in which the Guru was whole-sole responsible for the enlightenment of their students. Nobody even complained regarding lack of facilities in schools. We accepted whatever we got and getting knowledge was the prime goal to fulfil.

The time has changed now. The teachers can't even touch the student in spite of the constant nuisance created by the students because they are always in fear of getting suspended or terminated even when a false case is registered. I had never seen such a scene during my school days. It is not only in term of corporal punishment but in many domains the schools have become a different look far from the past. Double and triple storied buildings, facilities of modern labs, libraries, sports facilities, computer labs, mid- day meal facilities, well maintained parks, etc. All these present a glamorous look to schools. If you ask an elderly person that had he ever thought of such schooling facilities available to almost everyone during his school days- the answer definitely will be- 'No', as such facilities were rarely available and no one used to care about such facilities.

A common proverb which is often said- something never changes. I find it absolutely true as something has never changed from my school days to till present time and not only running parallel with time but has been developing with each day. These are- bunking of classes, truancy and bullying. These problems were in their initial stage then and now have flourished. The question is- Why do students bunk classes, drop out of school between their studies and get involved in bullying? These are burning issues and need to be sorted out. Efforts are going on to handle such issues properly and effectively to uproot these problems. Government along with administrators, educators and NGOs are trying their best to resolve these issues. In this regard, the efforts are going on to spread awareness to make the school environment much better for the betterment of each student. In spite of so much effort, problems are still existing because only facilities cannot replace the mindset of children. These happenings are due to the outburst of aggression in which the ratio of fear is much more involved. Let us go in detail to find out some facts.

School is a platform for the children where not only knowledge is imparted but it also facilitates the children to bring out their potential in a right and creative way. Facilities are the same for everyone and there is no partiality. It requires dedicated effort on part of children to develop their knowledge and personality under the guidance of teachers. In this process, some students are unable to cope up with the situation due to their carelessness and a time comes when such students break down. They face a dilemma in continuing their study and trying to uplift performance or dropping out from the school. Some of them become victims of bad habits and start smoking etc. The parents forcefully send them to school to make their future better. Though they come to school but cannot focus on studies and in extracurricular activities. It is a common theory that who performs better, he is appreciated and whose performance is not upto the mark, though he is not humiliated but he fully understands that he is being neglected. The students bunk classes as they do not find themselves comfortable in the classrooms due to their unwillingness in study and they leave the school. Though the fear of being neglected is their own perception, it destroys their schooling. The same case is with bullying. The bullies are the children who have been ever victim of someone else or trying to hide their own fear by showing themselves stronger than others. These problems are happening due to fear of adaptability in required situations.

The slogan 'work is worship' can be seen everywhere in the offices, workplaces, etc. which shows the importance of work. Are we dedicated enough to our assigned work? If 'yes' then why are there heaps of pending work awaiting and if 'No' then again who is responsible for the pending works? If anyone frequently visits the offices and other workplaces, he will definitely witness the various shades of workmanship that happens there when the people are independent to do work on their own and in other situations when their work is supervised and inspected by higher authority. I don't mean to say that people are committed to their work only when they sense danger of losing their jobs. All people are not equally faithful to their work and no one can deny this truth. It is human nature that a person puts hundred percent effort for his individual achievement and family related works but the same person doesn't contribute even fifty percent when it comes to collective work. Reason- the intensity of fear is more in accomplishing self work as it is directly related to him while in collective work the responsibility is related to group so the intensity of fear is less.

There is a huge difference between discipline and self discipline. Self- discipline is an awaking state of mind in which people are self motivated to follow the rules and regulations which are vital parts of their duty. They are indulged in the completion of their work honestly. On the other hand, discipline is maintained by ordering the people to follow rules and regulations and in order to fail, fear of punishment is always there. There are few people who understand the importance of self- discipline and for the rest, discipline is imposed to run the system smoothly and effectively. The people who don't follow these rules are always in danger of suspension or termination from their jobs. A few people work for their satisfaction while most people work for earning livelihood. Money plays a vital role in functioning our lives and it is earned through the world of work. Even the thought of losing a job creates fear and when it happens due to people's own fault then it becomes a very disgraceful situation. In reality, it occasionally happens that anyone becomes a victim of such a situation but, because it has happened in the past, it might happen anytime and the past incidents, especially bad ones, always generate fear.

I often find people telling a lie which doesn't harm anybody as they tell a lie to hide some facts which are related to their social reputation. It is regarded as an art to release pressure even for a moment. I would like to mention such an incident when I was in school studying in perhaps sixth or seventh standard. On a holiday, I was busy as usual in accomplishing my homework as it was part of my daily routine. My classmate's father was also present there and was indulging in gossiping with elderly people. In the meanwhile, the topic shifted on the academic performance of their wards and he told others that his son had scored maximum marks in the class. He looked very happy. I was amazed to hear as I was fully aware of his son's marks. Though I remained silent before him, I told my family members the truth as soon as he left. Everybody realized that the father was known to the fact but he said it to uplift his false pride. I could not believe it and became very curious to know the reason but didn't go to ask my classmate at once and waited for the next day.

As soon as I reached the school, I searched for him and found him in the playground. I asked him about his marks and he told his real marks honestly. Then I told him about the incident of the previous day and questioned him for not telling the truth to his father. He opened up and said that he had informed his mother. His father's behaviour was very aggressive so his mother thought that if he would tell the truth to his father, he might get into trouble. Keeping in view the peace of family, she suggested her son to skip away with truth. Though I was not able to understand the whole issue yet I realized that he did it due to fear. We can understand such a situation and have sympathy towards the sufferer and accept the fact that children tell a lie due to fear of being humiliated and punished.

Another such incident confirms that fear is one of the main reasons behind telling a lie. It happened when I had just joined my service and went to a wedding ceremony. I met a distant relative and he informed me that his elder son has been selected for civil services.

I was very pleased as his son was senior to me and was trying hard to get a job and was about to overage. After three or four months later his son came to meet me and I came to know that he was still unemployed. Such incidents raise so many questions. His father told lies due to social fear. He wanted to show false pride that he was the father of an administrative office. Fear forces people to lie. People are frequently hiding the truth due to fear of losing social prestige. Such practices are very harmful as when we come to know the truth, the concerned person feels guilty.

Generally, people are blind followers of their rituals and traditions. They don't want to argue in this regard, just follow the pattern which has been a part of their family tradition. Whenever someone tries to disobey these traditions, he is forced by elders to follow. Why do people force someone to follow certain traditions? If you ask this question to elders, each one will give a valid reason which will be supplemented with instances from the past. It is a general theory which is often used by the revolutionary people of our surroundings that rules are there to be scrutinized from time to time and changes are necessary to make them more useful. In this process, if by chance any mishappenings occur, then people believe that this is due to not following the traditions and some hidden force have become angry and they are punishing us. Some people call it a myth but no one can deny that it plays a big role in our life. All sections of people accept it as it comes their way.

It is a very common and ancient belief that when we are unable to fulfil our wish as our own, we pray to God to fulfil the wish. The most interesting thing in this process is that we assure him of bribes by promising to donate something after the successful completion of our wish. Seems funny but true. One side we are asking Him as he is almighty and on the other hand, we think ourselves capable enough to please him through certain things. In reality, only true devotion is needed. When the wish is fulfilled, people show their gratitude and donate whatever they promised earlier. Sometimes when people delay in accomplishing their promise, they always fear that the worst might happen. God is our creator. He never does injustice to us. Actually, the fear is due to insecurity.

People fear losing whatever they possess and which they consider precious for them. They never want to lose it and thus they are caught in the grip by the shadow of fear.

We all know that death is a universal truth. From the day we are incarnated on this planet, each moment brings us closer and closer towards it. The question is- how many people are there who are ready to accept the truth? Generally, no one wants to think about it as fear of death paralyzes even the strongest and the most intelligent person. It is very clear that we are here for a certain time period. The concept of immortality is an illusion. Man is mortal and it should be accepted as an ultimate truth. We often come across it in our day to day life, hearing from some people that they are not afraid of death but they become one of the weakest people whenever death passes near to them. Why do we fear death? It often occurs in mind that when people are well aware of this fact that life is for a limited time and we have to leave this planet after completion of our time still they don't accept this truth.

You can often see in your family or surroundings that whenever someone raises a topic related to death be it for a discussion or about any person, particularly elders intervene and stop to do so any further discussion about it. When they are unable to tolerate discussion about death, how can it be painful to face the reality of death? There are numerous reasons behind fear of death. There are certain responsibilities for each one in life. Everyone tries his best to accomplish his duties and responsibilities throughout his/ her life. It is very strange but true that a person does not fear for their own life much but does fear more for the lives of their loved ones. As everybody knows that one day, he has to leave but they want to fulfil all their desires and ambitions which are in various forms and these are never ending. Whenever people see such pathetic scenes of losing dear ones, the intensity of fear increases in multiple ways. Actually, desires are boundless. People want to live a happy life completely free from sorrow but life never permits. Such incidents are one of the many realities of life. Sometimes such incidents become very devastating which are intolerable. We witness such happenings through the media and feel a wave of fear. Imagine about the sufferers, it becomes very difficult for them to console themselves.

We believe in the theory of rebirth of soul. A soul has to be reincarnated one after another till he gets salvation from birth and death. In this process, we have to take birth in various forms on the basis of our deeds (karma) of our past life. We only know about salvation whatever we read in religious books and it means after getting salvation, we are free from birth and death. In the present scenario, when people come across these things one witnesses the cruel fate of life, their mindset diverges and they begin to believe in the theory of karma. People are afraid of punishment on the basis of their 'Karma' after death. So, fear of punishment for wrong deeds after death remains throughout life though most of time in hidden form.

We find that some people are scared of sending their wards to study in far off cities. A lot of doubts come in their mind and out of those doubts few are indeed baseless which are related to protection, fooding and lodging facilities. The real fear consists of insecurity and they do not want to be separated from their children. On the other hand, some people are very liberal in this regard. They allow their wards to go even abroad for studies and jobs keeping in mind the bright future of their wards. The question is- What is the reason behind different perceptions? The answer is- perhaps it is just a compromise for the benefit of their wards. They feel that they are fulfilling not only their ward's dreams but their own dreams also. But the fear of separation is always there and they anxiously wait for their safe return.

Pandemic COVID-19 and natural calamities such as earthquakes and tsunami bring havoc to mankind in every sphere of life. It has been found that most of the people die because of stampedes as fear suddenly creeps in everyone's mind and they are unable to react as they should have. A lot of efforts have been put in this regard as part of disaster management to train and alert the people to save themselves in such a situation. There is a huge difference between theory and practicality. When a person is caught in the realm of fear, he loses his sense to act accordingly.

Terrorism has become a burning issue. It can be commonly seen everywhere easily that people are forced to migrate due to the fear of terrorism. Imagine, how difficult it is? It is a real fact that no one wants to leave his/ her birth place in spite of some basic problems. Their main motto is to solve the problem and stay there. The love and respect for their birthplace always remains in their hearts. If they have to leave it because of earning livelihood but given a chance, they are always ready to visit their birthplace. The people are migrating and are happy to live in a very worse condition as fear of terrorism always exist in their mind and they don't want to go to their birth place but memories are always there. Heart is always willing to visit but the fear in mind stops it from doing so.

The range of fear is so vast that it includes our every action. Though the people want to get rid of it but are hopeless and most of the time it affects them badly. Its consequences are unable to heal easily and sometimes stings throughout life. During my Senior Secondary Schooling, one of my classmates who was also my close friend, used to fear that in spite of his consistent hard work, he would not be able to score good marks in class twelfth board examination. He developed this approach from the first term result of class eleventh. His belief was based on his own assumption. He was very much dedicated and used to spend a lot of time studying. We often used to visit each other's homes. Whenever he uttered such negative feelings to me. I used to ask him, "Why do you think so, you might not get your desired result each time but it's sure you will get it sooner or later as hard work always rewards." He used to smile at my preaches but never opposed as he had a lot of respect for me. The time went on passing and after our class twelfth board exam it was not possible to go to each other's home but whenever I got a chance to interact with him, I always found a glimpse of uncertainty in his eyes and face.

He could not perform as he wanted to. After the declaration of result, he was very dejected. I consoled him and asked him to pursue graduation with me. He obliged.

After graduation I had to leave the city due to some reason and came back after four years. I enquired about him and came to know that he left his study after completing graduation and now settled with his family in Mumbai. I was amazed as during these years I was there too and he was quite familiar but did not try to meet me. Sometimes our life does not permit us to do whatever we want. I could not go there due to my course and then because of my job. Suddenly destiny provided me a chance to go there and I was determined to meet him. Anyhow I managed to get his telephone number. It was the contact number of his elder brother so still I could not talk to him. I sent him information and went to visit his home. I reached there and found him absent. His wife and son welcomed me. They treated me as if they had known me for a long time even though I was seeing them for the first time. During the refreshment, his wife told me that my friend used to talk about me frequently and had great respect for me. His absence was a surprise to me. I asked, "Is there any important work for him and when will he come back? She honestly replied, "He doesn't want to face you" I was shocked. In disbelief I asked, "Why?" She told me, "he considers himself 'failure'. You always believed him and encouraged him but he could not fulfil your faith which you have always shown in him so he does not have courage to face you." I was speechless.

This incident tells itself that the roots of fear are very deep in our life. Fear of failure always moves in parallel as life goes ahead. People are unable to forget the fear of failure as it leads towards social humiliation and rejection. It is not a case with a single individual. It is a common problem and a large number of people are affected. Failure does not always come due to lack of effort. Actually, some people are not confident enough to do well in their particular fields such as- academics, sports, official work or any other actions. Though they do hard work to get through but in the meanwhile they are always in doubt about achieving their goal. The doubts always remain while practicing and it creates havoc during real situations. Once a doubt comes to mind and questions about one's own ability and potential, the performance is always in danger. It often happens that a student prepares very well for his course but sometimes he forgets it in the examination hall and once this happens, whenever such a situation arrives, the past experience is always there in the form of fear. It keeps on reminding him that such a situation might happen again.

In live performances such as sports and stage programmes, the intensity of fear of failure is very high. A person has to perform in front of a large audience. His or her performance is seen and inspected by all of them. There is always risk. If anyone does as per potential then his fear reduces in coming time as he becomes habitual of facing pressure. Sometimes unfortunate incidents occur. People are unable to handle pressure and so falter. This leads towards humiliation which is very painful to accept. Winning and losing is part of life. The most important fact is the way of handling the moment by each individual. Some take it as usual and channelize their fear into hard work for the next attempt but everyone cannot do the same. Some people break down as they are unable to cope up the pressure which is developed by our negative thinking and surroundings. It is a general tendency of people that they seldom discuss anyone's success but they endlessly talk about someone's failure and it is the real pressure which is very difficult to face.

Fear is a natural process which arrives automatically as people fear anything that is higher than them or what they can't control. It comes in many shapes and forms but can be described as an unpleasant feeling of perceived risk. The biggest problem with fear is that it exists in our minds. The mind conjures it up to protect itself from situations that it believes to be painful. Thus, it instils fear to turn us back from the situation that we are about to enter into. No one is willing to give it even a small corner in their life but by itself fear acquires the centre stage sometimes.

FEAR AS IT PROPAGATES– AN INTERACTION WITH REALITY

Whenever I say "I fear", friends laugh at me, family members look at me in disbelief as I am the eighth wonder of the world. The closest friends make a mockery by saying- "So, you fear". My answer is always plain as ever- "Yes" and this time in a broad perspective- "not only I, you too fear". "How can you say"? They ask, imposing seriousness. My answer is the same again- "Yes mate, we do, we are a part of a family and if we don't fear for ourselves then definitely for our loved ones". I continue- "Can you even pretend yourself to be fearless when anyone of your dear ones is struggling in the realm of danger. I don't hope so. Reason whatever may be but ultimately we fear."

At this juncture, I wait for their reaction but I find that most of the time, they just keep silent and don't respond. Perhaps recalling their memories of fearful moments and sometimes agreeing with me - "Yes, you are right". Actually, without accepting the truth we cannot take a step forward in the right direction so first and foremost it is very necessary for us to realize the horizon on which we are standing.

It is a universal truth that fear plays a key role in destroying the natural potential that people have than anything else on this earth. Everyone is capable of accomplishing incredible things. A happy life is available for each one on this planet. We are not able to achieve for which purpose we are here because fear in its many forms creeps in to ruin any chance at achieving our true greatness. Though most of our fear might not come true but do a tremendous amount of damage as we allow them to dictate ourselves and in this process they stop us from taking action. Fear of rejection, confrontation and loss keep us from taking new things. There is always a degree of risk that things might not go as we have planned. Now, I am trying to evaluate different aspects of fear which I have witnessed throughout my life.

The reign of fear is so vast and it rules over almost every aspect of our life such as- physical, mental, emotional, psychological, social, behavioural, spiritual and most important on performance which creates fear of failure- the most destructive one. Physical fear is well known. It can be identified easily in a stimulating situation. The symptoms of physical fear are more in a demonstrative way rather than in hidden so if we observe, we can easily get it everywhere in form of shaking legs and hands during delivering speeches in from of publics, increased perspiration, rapid heart beats, shallow rapid breathing, a queasy stomach, muscle tension, face turning pale, thirst and so on. Though at first look all these physical fears appear momentary and people feel that they can get over it easily but the impact is permanent in some cases. The person who has been a victim of such a situation can tell better than any other else. The trauma he has faced, he never forgets. The humiliation of that particular moment always remains just like a bad dream.

Ever been chased by a dog? You might have noticed that you stop only after covering a sufficient distance and feel that you are in a safe zone. Your physical indication of fear such as- rapid heart beat and continuous perspiration are telltale signs of the trauma you have been through. On the contrary, sometimes people are so terrified that they are unable to react physically and tend to become motionless. It's almost as if the brain freezes and everything stands still. This often is the aftermath of an unpleasant news which comes as a shock to individuals and is very tough to bear. These physical symptoms might fade away after the stressful event but the out-turn of these events on our mental health is significant.

Fear is also linked to underlying feelings that have been stamped out previously and later manifest themselves in the form of varied emotions. The tenure as to how long these feelings have been suppressed differs and the reaction is almost proportional to it. The greater the feelings have been suppressed for, the greater is the fear and wider the range of emotions. A rant from the boss causing us to fulminate against one of our co-workers to denying an opportunity consistently because of the fear of being deemed as incapable since you were a child by a member of the family aptly narrates the range.

Have you ever witnessed someone shouting for no reason

which often leaves people wondering the cause of their agitation? In reality, expressing different range of emotions such as anger, exasperation, agitation, lack of concentration, yelling for no reason, inability to make eye contact, lack of tolerance, inability to cope with certain environments, low motivation at work and the list goes on are directly or indirectly related to the mental aspects of fear . This is a cumulative effect of the past experiences which are painful and the wish for them to not be repeated again in future. This feeling of being perpetually terrified that these undesired events might happen again leads to a compounding fear, a kind that stays with us unless faced and tackled effectively. In the process of putting a barrier to such unwanted situations from happening again, we express emotions of frustration, agitation and anger which work against us. Our thought process is related to our minds, so when we are indulging in any task, our past memories trace any congruence and become active and communicate us our past experiences. It is then our level of resilience, courage, desire and ability to cope that decides whether we will part ways with our fear for good or have to stay with it for a considerable amount of time.

One explanation comes from Darwin's theory of evolution. During one of his visits to the London Zoo, Darwin decided to conduct an experiment. He started pressing his face as close as possible to the thick glass separating him from a poisonous puff adder. He found that every time the snake would lunge at him, he would instinctively jump back several feet.

Darwin derived a conclusion that despite our reasoning

powers, human beings continue to react in accordance with their primitive instincts which is primarily known as the fight-or-flight response-a physiological reaction to perceived threats which is designed to prepare an animal to either flee from danger or fight it.

While we are usually not faced with the threat of ravenous beasts waiting to eat us alive, we are faced with other modern-day perils--such as losing our reputations and not being accepted--which can lead to missing out on important opportunities. These possibilities are scary enough to trigger a fight-or-flight response in our bodies, causing all the outward symptoms we dislike so much: knots in our stomach, sweaty palms, a racing heart beat, dry mouth, shaky legs, slouched shoulders, a tightening throat.

Would it surprise you to know that the most powerful speakers we see today had a fear of public speaking? Quite a few notable speakers, leaders and performers have feared speaking or performing in front of large crowds--and have overcome it. If they can, so can you!

Although there is no dedicated strategy to cope with fright, there are ways to deal with it and even trick your body into believing that you are in a safe zone.

If there's one success story that can dispel your doubts about the untapped potential of fearful speakers, it's the story of Warren Buffett's opulent career.

Once a college student who was "terrified of getting up and saying [his] name," Buffett was able to overcome his aversion to speaking in front of others by facing his fears head on.

It was not easy, though.

He spent much of his college years avoiding courses that would require him to speak in front of the class. At one point, he mustered the courage to sign up for a public speaking course but then dropped out at the last minute.

At the age of 21, Buffet commenced his career as a stock broker and pretty much instantly realized that he had two alternatives: either force himself to face his fears or avoid them and never achieve his full potential. Buffett finally decided to take the first path and enrolled in a Dale Carnegie course on public speaking. He had a sigh of relief when he discovered that there were 30 other people in the class who were experiencing the same anxieties but were able to complete the course with flying colors. More often than not, fear of failure or any kind for that matter makes us believe that we are undeserving and worthless. The triumphant stories of these successful geniuses are a testament that we are not alone in our journey of discovering fear, getting acquainted with it and eventually overcoming it.

On the other hand, few of us fail to see the initial struggle and only notice the glorified version of their current success. What we fail to realize is that these victorious figures have been on a similar journey of fear and that their initial jitters are no different than ours.

As Buffet rightly said in one of his interviews "You have to do it. And the sooner you do it, the better. It's so much easier to learn the right habits when you're young. If you have a fear of associating with people, you have to go out there and do it, and it's painful...,".

Buffet's story is indeed a dynamic one but not the only one. Take Thomas Jefferson for example.

A spokesman for democracy, was an American Founding Father, the principal author of the Declaration of Independence and the third President of the United States had his own share of fears.

Despite his fears, he still became a Founding Father of America, an impassioned defender of democracy and the main author of the Declaration of Independence.

Some of you would be surprised to know that the instances of Jefferson's drastic fear—often talked about in his biographies and other historical documents--are so grave that psychiatrists have even diagnosed him with social phobia.

The second president of the United States, John Adams, for example, noted that he never witnessed Jefferson utter more than three sentences together during his tenure that he served with him in Congress.

Remarkably, he only gave two public speeches during his eight years as President--both of them inaugural addresses. According to those present, they were delivered in such a low tone that they could hardly be heard. One of his biographies also observed that whenever Jefferson attempted to shout, his voice would "sink in his throat."

Although it is not fully known as to how Jefferson ever really overcame his fears of speaking in public, he most definitely made himself capable enough to successfully work his way around his shortcomings by relying mostly on his exceptional writing abilities. This brings us to another important part- "focusing on our strengths rather than our shortcomings and using it to our advantage.

You all must be familiar with the name of the renowned author "Stephen King". Most of us know him as a bestselling author with more than 80 over books to his accolade. But what many of us might not know is that his journey to success was not an easy one. King went through his own share of hardships and rejections.

He worked several low-paid jobs before landing a teaching job at a local high school. From tackling the shackles of poverty to being on the verge of giving up after multiple rejections, he witnessed it all. He even ended up throwing pieces of his writing in the trash until his wife pulled the pages out and encouraged him to keep going and not give up. After putting in his full efforts Stephen King finally completed his first book. Following this, he was in for a lot of rejections. He sent it out to a list of publishers and received a similar response. With the amount of rejections he faced, he was drowning in an array of despondency but he still didn't let go of his perseverance and kept trying. While you would expect any other person to give up in a situation like this, King believed in himself and kept trying, thereby overcoming his "fear of rejection".

His consistent efforts yielded results when one day everything changed. One of the publishing houses agreed to publish his book and pay him some money. Though it was not a lot of money, it surely meant something as his family was on the brink of poverty. When "Carrie" was finally published, it sold over a million copies in its first year. This was the major breakthrough and his life took a major turn post that. Despite the several setbacks and failures, Stephen put in his hard work and turned the tables successfully. There was also a time in his life where he suffered from severe addiction to alcohol and other drugs. But with proper help and care, he became sober and continued to write. The several hurdles and failures in King's case were walked past with persistent hard work.

Stephen King is a personification of a person who didn't let failure define him. He could have easily kneeled before the failures but he didn't let his rejections define him. He got back every single time and worked even harder. His success and overcoming his failure was possible due to his belief in himself and the perseverance to keep trying and never giving up. And that is something that sets us apart from the rest. We should never let "the fear of failure" take over our success. Our ability to keep going and having enormous faith in our abilities will lead us to our destination despite the hurdles. Yes, the road is going to be long and bumpy but don't we appreciate things even more when we have seen the worst?

If there is one simple mantra to taste the sweet essence of success, it is to never let your failures define you, rather let them be a lesson and not let them deter you to keep moving towards the right direction. Much to our dismay, some past painful experiences make a rather permanent place for themselves in our minds and the shadow of the past cripples us from taking a step in the right direction or even doing the bare minimum, i.e. trying.

During my initial counseling sessions, I came across a lot of incidents where teenagers and young adults would refrain from taking any action just because a similar circumstance in the fast has led to unfavorable consequences.

The list of these issues seemed endless and overwhelming. From not disclosing their relationships with their parents for the fear of abandonment or inability to pursue a career of their choice as it wasn't considered conventional as per the societal norms, it was heartbreaking to see the kids go through such enormous constraints at such a tender age. The root cause of all this? FEAR!!

As cliche as it may sound, the fear of what others think, the fear of not fulfilling others' expectation or not being good enough for others has crushed and continues to crush our own dreams, aspirations and even little joys of our day to day life. If we take a moment to introspect to get into the root cause of these fears, we will realise that maybe all of us had a role to play in inculcating fears like these not only in ourselves but also others. You may wonder how? Let me break it down for you.

Yes many of us grow up and evolve and even repent any act that we might have done in the past. But the real learning will be "UNLEARNING". Unlearning to judge people for the most trivial things, Unlearning to pass a casual remark on any random individual looking seemingly fine but might be fighting their battles, unlearning to not give others a hard time if we are not feeling our 100%, unlearning to stop saying yes to things we are incapable of and the list goes on. . . . Instead, "LEARN", learn to be kind, to be compassionate, learn that if we can go through tough times, the other person could too, learn how important it is to UNLEARN the stereotypical ideologies and the mindset we have thrived in and LEARN to change it. Change and learning is infectious and as rightly said, "Be the change you want to see in the world".

For every person we have knowingly or unknowingly judged which might have led to them wondering, whether or not they are good enough- We need to change that. If we have been on the other side, then we need to understand that somebody else's opinions of us don't depict who we are. No matter how mighty we allow fear to become- the solution lies at the minute level,i.e. your thoughts, your minds. Maneuver your thoughts in the direction of positivity, self worth and resilience and be an amazed spectator of the changes it brings to you.

The roots of negativity, doubts, despair or baseless anxiety are pitted deep into the illusive world of psychological fear. We often romanticize pain and fear leading to building up scenarios which exist only in our imaginations. It shows that psychological fear is a state of mind and gradually becomes reality for the concerned person. Fear always dwells in people's mind in its abstract form but what really gives it a shape and identity is the magnitude of our thoughts and actions.

"Oh I didn't receive a text from her today, there must have been something wrong with my behavior that pushed her away". . . . "He didn't seem himself in the class today, he was behaving strangely and didn't seem interested in me". . . . "I shouldn't have put forth my idea during the presentation, everyone must have thought I'm such an amateur, I'm never doing this again". . . . " Why would she speak to someone like me, I should never tell her how I feel" . . . .

You see? You'd be lying to yourself if you haven't had these or similar thoughts. Studies show that the average person has about 12,000 to 60,000 thoughts per day. Yeah mate, you heard (read) that right. . . . Mind boggling, isn't it?????

You know what's even more mind boggling??? 80% of them are negative and 95% are repetitive thoughts. . . Crazy, I know!!!!

Now think about the huge ripples your mind creates when you couple these negative thoughts which are repetitive. It's like asking for trouble. What we need to understand is that our thoughts hold power. They are made up of memories, our perceptions, our beliefs. They are fragments of ideas.... Our thoughts determine the orientation of everything we do. They evoke the feelings that frame our world and motivate our actions. And they have the power to change the way we feel. And since the way we feel has a direct correlation to our emotions, fear being one of the seven universal emotions experienced by us-our thoughts hold a great power in instilling fear.

Whenever something doesn't seem to be going right, it's easy to feel that we must have been in the wrong. Sorry for saying it out loud but try getting into a millennial's mind and good luck finding your way out. Our minds, for the lack of a better terminology are messed up in the truest sense. From wanting a stellar professional life to finding the love of our lives while striking a balance, we want it all. On paper, all of it seems ideal or may I say achievable? But in reality, don't even get me started. . . . .

The fear of getting judged, ridiculed and rejected are some of the most common fears we live with. I have said that again and I'll say it again- the only change we need to bring about is in our "thoughts" because this marks the inception of fear at the very fundamental level. So, the next time we are ready to jump onto a bandwagon of self-doubt and self-criticism if things are not going our way, how about we pause for a second and "reflect". We need to understand even if we have such fears such as fear of abandonment and in the worst case scenario, even if it does come true, we need to understand that we are bigger than this. Someone else's decisions have nothing to do with who they are and it shouldn't deter us from trying or being in a similar situation again.

It is very important to remember this: If we make the mistakes, we learn and if we are on the receiving end of someone else committing mistakes, then also we learn. We learn to let go, to forgive, to thrive and to begin again!

So, the next time you are trying to take control of the situation by over analyzing and overcompensating through unnecessary actions, control your thoughts and break the cycle then and there.

As it must be clear by now that a lot of psychological fear stems out of negativity. When we deem ourselves incapable to face a particular situation, that's when fear lurks in. Fear is well aware that the best time to capture our mind is when it is at its weakest, when it isn't guarded by a positive light or signs of hope. It grasps us in its clutches when we are at our most vulnerable. And this is why I keep emphasizing how important it is to tame your thoughts in the positive direction.

Negative thinking hampers our ability to see and analyze the possibilities that the present situation beholds, thereby hindering our abilities to carve a way out. The most menacing aspect of psychological fear is that it prevents people from taking initiative. As it freezes our ability to think and act, we become hopeless and the mere spectators of our own misery. The negativity of mind always diverts it towards the dark side of life, towards the things that are perceivably not going right. When the mind conjures up all the petrifying developments and is convinced that it is going to culminate into a daunting reality, this becomes a recurring pattern and hence a part of a person's nature.

The question is what can be done to change it? Is there someone else who can help us get through our fears? Yes, it is indeed true that self-motivation is the key to conquer our fears but a little push from the right individuals could go a long way too. It's like an icing on the cake. Our social circle is a part of our entity- the things we discuss, the conversations we share is like fodder to our mind. In short, it does tend to leave a mark on us. We would often accept to surround ourselves with like-minded people and people who uplift us but is this always the case?

Probably not. . . . .Where do you think one of our biggest fears- "fear of abandonment" stems from. Why do we fear so much within our social groups? What is this dormant fear that's lodged within those minds amidst smiling faces and enchanting conversations? Let us address the elephant in the room.

Up until now we have only heard fancy words like "social pressure" or "peer pressure" but never tried to get into the root cause of it and the kind of fear it propagates. Funny to think our efforts to be social stems out of our fear of being abandoned. What an irony!

Everyone's ambition is to be loved, known and establish a respectable place for them in their respective social groups. From very early on, we witness the social pressure and gradually understand that in spite of living in the same society, a lot of difference exists in terms of getting the success, respect, honour and social prestige that one receives. Most of us are trying to be what is deemed as the best as per norms. Nobody wants to be second to others. It seems as if everyone wants to be better than the others rather than the best version of themselves. Ever wondered why?

The problem is that we are constantly judged by others and judge others and amidst the rat race, start losing our own entity as an individual trying to imbibe the best from everyone else's. While there's nothing wrong in being inspired but negating your own strengths to follow someone's own doesn't seem like a good starting point. This is wear your fear of losing out or fear of missing out, FOMO as the millennials like to call it starts creeping in.

We are constantly being monitored and scrutinized by the people around us or so we think, which makes it worse. In extreme cases, it gets to a point where it seems arduous to just be yourself. The huge discrepancy between our real lives and social media, the inexorable desire to go out our way to please others, the inability to stay on just to fit in etc etc..... just goes on to show how "fear of not fitting" is taking away from us our uniqueness and more often than not, our mental peace.

It is true that when we are living in a society, it is important to socialise and mingle. But the detail we miss out on is that it is important to socialise with the right set of folks. Folks who inspire you, uplift you and motivate you in your endeavors. While it's okay to socialise, it is not okay to socialise for the sake of it. Take time finding your own niche, people who match your frequency and reciprocate the energy and efforts that you put in. Don't rush in trying to fit in, else you'll always fear being out of place and any safe social circle is not characterized by fear but a safe place where you can connect, grow and openly communicate.

IS FEAR UNIVERSAL?– HORIZON OF FEAR

Have You ever witnessed in your day to day life such a scenario - a group of youths laughing at weak and fragile characters, making fun of them by calling names- timid, cowardly, fearful, etc. People stop for a while, see it, smile and go away. I don't only hope but quite assured that you have witnessed such a situation. We all know that change is the law of nature. Nothing is permanent or for granted on this planet so, the situation as above mentioned can't be remained forever for a particular person. Though characters might be the same, the sufferer may differ. The humiliation and the pain remains the same.

Since the rise of human civilization, the concept of fear has arrived in human beings' lives. Now, the question is not here about the existence of fear as it has already been proved and accepted. The question is regarding the range of fear. As there is such a vast difference among the capacity of people. As someone has climbed on the top of Mount Everest while others are thinking about starting their journey towards the top and are roaming in frustration while searching for the way. I don't mean to applaud here the adventurous achievement of someone and the weakness of others through this comparison. I only mean to find out if the person who is standing at the top has ever felt fear during his journey to reach there or while making a lay out plan for this adventurous journey.

I often see people who are deprived of the so- called high profile facilities lamenting about their pathetic condition. They forcefully blame their condition for their feeling of insecurity, tension, anxiety, etc. and all symptoms of fear in which they are badly gripped in. It is their firm belief that a sound financial status combined with power can easily negotiate or even eradicate the fear.

Do you agree with their perception? The answer is being awaited but here, I am recalling some incidents of history and analyzing these with the context of the present scenario to get a clear picture in this regard.

Each human being is born on this planet for a certain time. It is a human tendency that most of the time they want to ignore this universal truth. Even the imagination of death creates fear. The fear of death or thanatophobia is a relatively complicated phobia and if not all but most people are afraid of the death. It is not in the case of rich or poor, caste, religion, etc. This fear has been very prevalent among people throughout the world. It may also have roots in the fear of the unknown. People are very curious to know regarding happenings after death. What happens after death, however, cannot be unequivocally proven while we are still alive. People who are highly intelligent or inquisitive are often at greater risk. The act of dying is utterly outside anyone's control. Those who fear loss of life try to hold death at bay through rigorous and sometimes extreme health checks and other medical procedures. Many people's fear of death is related to their religious beliefs as they think that they know what will happen to them after death as per their knowledge of religious literature but are also worried that they may be wrong. Some people believe that the path to salvation is so straight and narrow that any deviations or mistakes may cause them to be eternally condemned.

In some parts of our country, there is a tradition of reading 'Garun- Puran' by family members after anyone's demise in their family. Generally, a person reads and the rest of the family members and relatives listen attentively. During my childhood, I could not understand why a book was being read in the presence of so many people. The reason was that we used to read and recite 'RamcharitManas' together and it would be a function. But in the case of 'Garun Puran' the situation was different. I developed a curiosity in this regard to read this book. I got a chance to read religious books as they were easily available but still this particular book I could not get and the fact was, I didn't try hard enough also due to other priorities. Once I had to stay at my relative's house due to the demise of a family member. During the stay, I showed a keen interest in listening to Garun Puran. You will be wondering about my focus on Garun Puran but it has a valid reason. The journey of human beings after death is described in this book. The book describes that no one can escape at any cost and they will have to pay for their evil deeds. If you have done 'good Karma' then you are certain to get salvation and for ' evil deeds' such a life has been described that even for a moment, people are certain to take oath for never indulging in evil deeds. The interest towards life disappears.

It has been my own experience throughout my life. I have found people of all religion, caste, educated or uneducated, poor or rich believing that life is uncertain and this fear of death always remains. It proves the universality of the fear of death because we almost get many chances in life for anything but as for the present life, we have only one chance. Even the thought of feeling that we will not be able to see and help our dear ones fills us with fear. Since ancient times, yajnas were performed to protect life when people were known to be in danger. The performing of 'Maha Mrityunjaya yajna' can be seen frequently which is organized for the long life of a person. People can be seen praying for their own lives as well as dear ones in temples, gurudwaras, churches and mosques throughout the world. We often see people trying to save their lives during natural calamities, earthquakes, etc. We don't see it in any part of the world that some of them are standing there only and are not reacting to save themselves. It means that whenever anyone is caught in the reign of fear, he desperately wants to save his life. So, it proves that fear of death exists everywhere and each one is under its grip.

There is a craze of watching horror movies throughout the world. I think almost all people in all age groups like these movies. Horror serials are also being telecasted on various TV channels. Movies and TV serials which are based on the stories of ghosts, witches, spirits introduce us to a fascinating world of fear and our curiosity keeps on increasing. Generally, children and youth are very much interested as it provides them with a thrill and they see the amazing incidents which are sometimes beyond their imagination. These movies are often a huge hit. Not only horror movies and TV serials attract people, stories and books are also liked by people describing wonderful incidents which are related to fear. In this regard, I would like to mention Harry Potter- a fiction based on magical horror that created all records in earning money. It was due to people's eagerness to read out the book and see the various facets of the fear.

What is the reason behind people's attachment to watching horror movies? I have seen that even the children who are generally scared by nature, also show their keen interest in watching such films. Children often urge their grandparents to share the stories of magical powers, ghosts, etc. In my opinion, whatever we are unable to face and see in real life situations, we develop an interest and curiosity to see these as fictions. As we are quite aware of real danger which can happen facing such evil powers though it might be a mere assumption but the truth is that we are always told and cautioned through our elder members of the family. Whatever we have been informed during our childhood by senior members of our surroundings, we want to verify it as we grow and its roots develop since our childhood. Whenever we get a chance to peep, which has been in our concept for a long time, we tend to follow despite our hidden fear.

As we know, human nature is very strange and unique in seeking the truth. They have a deep desire to unveil the secret which has been eluding them for a long time and in this process, they become constantly involved whenever they sense something strange. Generally, most people don't want to take risks intentionally and willingly. Their hidden fear functions as a stimulus which prohibits them from going forward. There are only a handful who seldom care and often go in deep to find out the truth and are ready to face the danger. So, whenever people get a chance to see whatever they were deprived of in the past due to their own fear or because of the advice of their family members, they don't want to miss it now when the opportunity arrives. Their hidden desire prompts them to unfold the mystery without any possibility of danger. Even a child of ten years old is quite confident that whatever he is watching through movies, serials or reading in a book can never ever harm him at any cost. This safe side of life is a plus point for everybody to witness the extreme horror through movies, serials, etc. and know about it and in return it provides them amusement as well as pleasure.

But, it is true that the future's happenings are beyond our expectations. Everyone has his own way of tackling the situation. As in the above mentioned situations, people are completely assured that there is no harm done while watching the horror but it cannot be said exactly true. We tend to be involved physically, mentally and emotionally with whatever we come across. Though the effect cannot be seen easily, it cannot be denied totally. Particularly in the case of children, they are very much attached with whatever they see and feel. Their tender mind and heart would not be able to accept it as a fiction. They try to connect with the characters. Sometimes, in trying to repeat the act as performed in the movie, their lives are exposed to danger as we have seen in many cases. It is not the case of any particular section of society's children, it is related to all the children around the world.

If a question is asked- What is the most significant thing for the existence of life? Generally, people answer- food and water. On enquiring again - Are you sure? This time the answer might be more scientific as they will use their brain and will try to recall their memories whatever they are acquainted with during the study of science. Now, they might say- breathe, as it is true that we can survive a few days without food and water but cannot survive without taking a breath.

So, my friend, no need to puzzle. Try to accept the truth which is the ground reality. We are not born on this planet to live only for a few days without food and water. We are here to perform certain specific duties as human beings so for survival for a long period, food and water are our prominent requirements. That is the reason we often say that food and water are must for life and we often hear people saying- we work for bread. We all will definitely agree that financial crises create panic situations in our lives, even if we don't imagine it to happen to us even in our dreams. The fulfillment of the needs of our life revolves around money as each and everything which is needed for life in terms of facilities is purchased through money.

Now, the question is- What are the needs of human beings? Money is not required for only food, shelter and clothes but it plays one of the most important parts during the life span. Many children are deprived of higher education due to lack of money and some of them were one of the best students during the early part of their school life and were considered very promising. They were unable to prove their potential in the absence of resources and were forced to leave the study and unwillingly bound to support their families to earn livelihood.

There has been a huge gap among the people from the ancient time till present in terms of lifestyles. Who wants to live in a pathetic and hopeless situation ? Definitely no one. This is the reason why the financial crisis plays havoc in people's minds. Money is not only needed by people for only a lavish lifestyle and quality education, it is badly required sometimes to save the life of a person as the medical facilities are going beyond reach due to its continuously increasing costs. Though the government is trying its best, it is not enough. The lives of people are in danger as they are unable to pay for medical facilities. Imagine, how painful it is for a person to not be able to pay the amount for his/ her own life or his loved ones.

In this regard, I want to mention the social life of ancient times that was surrounded with religious beliefs. Whatever the facts are available, these show that the low financial status of people was almost the same as of today but there was a huge difference in the mindset. The people who did not have good financial resources believed that it was their misfortune that was related to their 'karma' of previous life. So, they were content with whatever they had, thinking it the grace of almighty and used to live happily in the same position. But, there is a drastic change in the mindset of people today. They are not ready to accept whatever they have. To some extent, it can be understood if their approaches are in the right direction to fulfill their financial ambition but it is not the case. They want to get it at any cost - fair or unfair means legal or illegal ways, they don't bother to think about it , just passionate enough to earn money.

The fear of financial loss or fear of not being able to generate financial resources have filled their mind and heart with fear. They want to survive in this glamour world and also want to acquire a prominent place for themselves in the society. They don't want to label themselves as 'failure' or 'poor' in their family or society and it leads them towards committing any wrong deeds to earn money.

We often watch TV news channels and read in newspapers about missing persons. Almost all people are victims of such incidents. If we see that a person who is missing is a normal guy, we generally think that he has gone somewhere due to some differences with his family and will come back. Imagine about the missing children who are not competent enough to understand the reality of the world. The trauma such children and their family members face is beyond imagination. It can be understood by people's cautious approach that whenever we go in public places, we always give instructions to our younger members to remain with the group. In case he/ she is separated then in place of going here and there in search for others, just stand and wait there and if possible, inform the police.

I have often heard the stories of missing children in the fairs and other crowded public places by elders. I always wondered how it was possible? The reason was based on the ground reality which I used to witness. Whenever I went to a crowded public place during childhood, I was always accompanied by elders. As it was the concept of elder members of the family that if the children would go alone at such places, the risk of certain to follow though it may or may not. The elders were constantly holding the hands of children due to fear of separation. But, despite so many cautious approaches, it often occurs. We find the children weeping due to fear of separation but the things are managed in most of the incidents. When a few minutes or a few hours separation is so painful and dreadful then the fear and trauma can easily be felt in the case of long term separation.

The incidents of children being kidnapped for the sake of money or taking revenge from the family have been more prevalent which we are witnessing in society and through the media. Such incidents were very rare in the past but are growing rapidly in the present time and happening all over the world and in all sections of society. The criminals and terrorists are using it as a weapon frequently. We see through the media even the hijacking of planes, buses carrying people to their destination. I mean to say that such heinous crimes are done not only for revenge or for money against a particular person but also at the mass level. Those few hours or days of captivity always left a scar in the minds of the victims that it takes a long time to heal. Even the people whose families were not in that plane or bus but they become emotionally attached with the victims and their families and feel the intensity of fear so much and get relieved after the situation becomes normal.

There is a hype of the glamour world among people and particularly in teenagers. They are very much fascinated about its outward brightness and don't bother to look deep to search out the real scenario. As we see, film stars and sportspersons who have been excellent and are blossoming in their fields are followed by large numbers of fans who are devoted to them. They want to look like them and try to copy them as much as possible. They forget that the roles played by film stars on the screen are fictional characters and as per the need of the story and not their real one.

They are also human beings and have to live life in the same way as others. The money and fame which have become their companions today are a reward of their potential which has come alive due to their hard work and some part of luck. The higher we climb in any field, the risk is bigger in sustaining that position as nothing is taken for granted. This develops fear of insecurity of declining from the position they are at the present moment. It is human nature that once you reach the pole position, you always fear that someone might replace you from this position as you have done by dethroning someone else.

Actually, the fact is when we are short of resources for the fulfillment of our basic needs as well as desires, we try our best to have it. If we are able to achieve, we want to keep this position throughout our life at any cost. As we know that we have earned it after overpowering many hurdles. We compare our life when in the absence of enough resources, it was difficult to survive and cope up the critical phases with the present one, in which everything is going on smoothly. As we have witnessed both the situations, fear of losing the current position is there as it has provided everything which has been a part of our dream.

There are instances in the history of dethroning kings sometimes by their own relatives and ministers. There was always fear of losing their kingdom, sometimes by the rulers of other kingdoms and sometimes by any insider within the surroundings. The rulers used to be very protective in terms of their own security and thus a lot of people were employed as bodyguards. The fear has established its roots in the political arena worldwide. In the present scenario, the security is being provided as per the positions and risk of the concerned politicians. People are forced to spend manual power and finance for their security. It is not the case of only an individual, it is everywhere. A huge amount of Budget of each country is being spent in upgrading defence forces and maintenance for the security of the country and its citizens. As a citizen, everyone wants to give his/ her contribution in the development and protection of the country. When we fear for our own security, society and country then we try our best with the resources available to protect.

So, a huge sum of resources of each country which could be

used in developmental programmes and uplifting the status of their citizens is being spent for the security of borders and interim security of the country. Where there is a fear of the protection of the nation, every sacrifice is considered vital and people are ready to give their contribution as much as they can. It is seen all over the world that not only in the present time but it has been in the past also. With the feeling of 'Freedom is our birth right', people develop love and respect for their country so they are ready to face challenges. Fear is the main reason behind the unity. It is good to be united though it is only for overcoming their hidden fear. Imagine, if there is no fear of security all over the world, then the social, economic and political situation would be like heaven.

Life has become very complicated. The interesting point is that we, ourselves make it complicated as we are rushing towards an endless road of collecting facilities for us and our families. We are leaving far behind the moral values which play an important role in making our life beautiful in spite of lack of financial resources. It is natural theory that we have to pay for each thing we get in our life. If we search for people who are completely free from nervousness, anxiety and tension and are living happily then I don't think that the journey of search would be easy.

In this regard, take the cases of people since their schooling period onwards. They are in tremendous pressure in terms of not only their academic performance but adjusting themselves as per the need of different situations also. The fear of failure continuously follows them class by class and after completion of study it becomes more dangerous as they are expected to convert their potential into their jobs. So, the pressure is present for each student but in different roles? The low achievers need to be performed as per their ability and potential and higher achievers are expected to maintain their position. The position of parents is the same as they sometimes are under more pressure than their wards. It is not a case of a particular society or a country, it is all over the world.

Tension and anxiety have become a never ending process of life as whatever we have achieved we don't get satisfied, always aspire for the next destination. Cordial relationships play an important part in our life- be it with our own family, social groups or at work places. People are so busy in achieving their goal that they are unable to keep a pace with their relationships as they should be. People are often caught in a dilemma. On the one hand, whatever they are trying to achieve is not only for their personal gain but for their families also and on the other hand it is soaring their relations.

It is a dream of every individual to reach at the top in every walk of their lives. The efforts are being put in throughout life in this regard as power, fame and money have become an integral part of people's life. Every living human being on this planet is trying to become the ultimate version of themselves, to show the highest capability and express individual uniqueness. In this process, they tend to feel pressure due to fear of failure and it is the condition of each one which shows the universality of fear and we see that the horizon of fear is spread throughout the world.

FEAR– A DISEASE OR A CONCEPTUAL STATE OF MIND

Friends, now it's time for a debate regarding the concept of fear. The topic - fear is a disease or a conceptual state of mind. I realized that my own experience is not quite enough to unfold the mystery as whatever I have seen in the realm of fear, it is not completely providing a clear view to reach at the conclusion. As I am blessed with meeting people of all sections of society, so, I decided to take the viewpoint of others in this regard. In this process, I came across the views and experiences of various intellectuals of their fields which include- administrators, lawyers, educators, engineers, bankers, doctors, psychologists, counsellors, students etc. It provided transparency in verifying the reliability of the samples/ data.

I don't completely believe in whatever has been already written as these are the views of few people which are based on their ideas and research works. World is so vast that it is almost impossible for a person to experiment his/ her innovative ideas with the whole population. He/ she does it on a particular group of his surroundings and in some cases the horizon could be a little wider. It is the need of the hour that when we want to get a clear picture on any issue, it is better and appropriate to collect the views of various intellectuals as their vast experiences can contribute a lot in this regard and also provide uniformity.

Politics, films and sports are the hot topics which are frequently discussed in all the arenas all over the world and are very popular among all age groups. People show enormous generosity and patience in spending their time while discussing these issues. But when someone tries to collect data on some serious topics such as fear, people generally are not interested and don't take it seriously. So, I was very cautious while collecting the data in terms of the above mentioned topic and tried to create an informal environment in order to get a natural response. It is a general human tendency that when the choices are given, it is easy to respond but when the answer with a logic is required then it is tough as it needs reliability and validity. In the process of their responses, all of them agreed that it is a conceptual state of mind but as the time progresses, it becomes a disease in such cases where the intensity of fear is increasing continuously and there is no sign of getting rid of the existing fear. They arrived at the conclusion that consistent presence of fear leads towards mental illness as it affects the thought process and slowly negativity of mind leads towards depression.

Now, in the perspective of all these processes my curiosity increased so on the basis of the collected data, I am integrating it with a few real life experiences which I have witnessed. It is my own opinion that many times, the analysis done by us is based on our assumption. Actually, in trying to make things in a very systematic way, somewhere it is possible that we might miss the originality, that is why the reliability and validity are required. It is my firm belief that real life experiences are very valuable assets to see things in the right perspective.

Case Study- 1, It is a story of an old woman who had two sons. She loved them so much and was very protective of them in all respects. Though her sons were married and they have their own children, she used to treat them as kids. She was not ready to accept that her sons were too old to get such protection. She was very happy to take responsibilities which were in fact her son's liabilities. She did not allow her sons to visit the places which she found harmful for them and always denied them to face troubles. Slowly and slowly it became her son's habit to avoid the challenges thrown at them. They had their own family but they were dependent on their mother during critical moments of life and always hesitated to take initiatives. They thought that they didn't have the capability to overpower the situation and always looked hopeless. As nobody is immortal in this world. After the demise of their mother one of them anyhow managed to make an adjustment with the proceedings of life but the other son found it very difficult as mother's attachment and protection was even greater for him.

As we know, life is a moving process. It does not stop with anybody's wish or inability to move. The condition of the younger son became very pathetic. He was clueless, unable to start to live in a normal way. There was no lack of resources but he was not competent enough to use the resources he had. The main problem was with him mixing up with others. He was afraid of being humiliated by others as he found himself unable to adjust with them. He used to avoid meeting people of dominant nature. Loneliness became his companion. His constant negative thinking began to reflect in his activities and became a part of his personality. His behaviour became abrupt and irritating and he was caught in depression.

In the above mentioned case study the mother's role may be held responsible for her son's pathetic condition at first glance. But, here we should see the things in a broad perspective. It can easily be observed that the mother's behaviour was an example of innocent extreme love and protection for her sons. Even though she was afraid to imagine trouble in her sons' lives, fear was always present in her love and protection. She was in a dilemma. Though she wanted a happy and prosperous life for her sons but due to her hidden fear she never allowed them to learn the art of survival which was a key for happy living. Anybody's ability and potential is tested in adverse conditions and teaches a lesson which is very useful in life. Her over protection deprived them of learning useful lessons of life. In reality, her negative approach became very harmful for her sons.

As we see, her attachment and protection was at extreme for her younger son so after her demise, he was completely hopeless. He was not a child, instead he had his own family to look after which he never realized before. He never imagined such a painful situation. He was habitual of his own protection by his mother and now he had to lead from the front for the sake of his own family. Now, he was compelled to face the challenges which his mother always avoided citing the issue of risk which were in his mind in the form of fear. So, he always withdrew and it became his habit. He could not cope up with the fear which might be faced if he would have shown courage to face the challenges. He chose the second option- to live with his fear and consistently increasing problems forced him towards depression.

Case Study- 2, it is a peculiar case of a boy aged around sixteen years old. The boy has a habit of showing himself very powerful in his surroundings. He is also good in studies and sometimes even shows enormous respect for elders of the society. The main point is that his behaviour is very fluctuating. Sometimes his behaviour appears abnormal and awkward. His friends are generally five to ten years old to him and his classmates are not his friends. He is very much pampered by his parents. Nobody likes the boy and his parents in the society in which his family lived. Though formality in behaviour exists there during social gatherings but trust is always missing and people just want to avoid them. The boy and his family desperately want respect from their society and want to be known as prosperous but the people of their society don't care much about them due to their past experiences and never show respect and importance to them.

Specially, people neglect the boy as he has developed such a strange habit of imbalanced behaviour that people often find it difficult to understand. His communication style becomes very absurd sometimes so people want to keep him away from their ward in order to save them from his company. They think that his companion might be harmful to their wards. At this age, he is quite old to understand all this. His parents also know the fact but pretend that it is not so. Actually, they are unable to accept the situation. Though they try to adjust their behaviour so that their son may get recognition from others but they are unable to control their habit also. Whenever people come to know about their abnormal behaviour, they term them 'mental' particularly to their son.

The case is all about living in a hypothetical state of mind. In order to stamp their superiority in the society they are part of, they are indulged in such an act that people don't trust them. Reputation is not a thing which can be purchased from the shop. It is earned through dedicated efforts by contributing his share or more than that for the welfare of the society or for an individual of the society in the time of need. It is the tendency of parents that whatever they are unable to get for themselves, they fear that their children might get the same fate. It creates fear in their minds. They want to get it for their wards by hook or crook but the situation is not in their hands. The unsuccessful attempt of hidden desires generates frustration. Though they try their best to deceive others by their artificial behaviour, it does not last long. People are smart enough. They sooner or later catch the intention of such people and their approach becomes very careful while dealing with such people.

In this case, the family and particularly the boy are not trying to adjust themselves as per normal behaviour instead they are doing their best to get it through manipulation whatever they want and the boy, in order to prove himself a strong character among his age group, joins the group of youths much older than him. They are clever enough to exploit the boy and use him for their own purpose. Thus, in order to fulfill his hidden desire to take control of others he often finds caught at fault. People make him responsible while others who are also involved in mischief yet they manage to escape due to their clean images.

In society, people label someone as 'mental' not because of their jealousy, it is due to their consistent analysis of anyone's frequent abrupt behaviour, initially they avoid it but later on begin to ignore the concerned person. This is the same situation as the boy mentioned here. He has lost faith in the people and is fully aware of it. He understands that people don't like or trust him. So, he has developed a habit of hiding the real facts from someone who is unaware about him due to the fear of losing respect and is well supported by parents but he gets the same fate as he is unable to control his mischievous behaviour for a long time. He is showing some symptoms of mental illness and it is surmounting due to tremendous pressure from ownself for his hidden desire to stamp his supremacy on others which is alluding him & fear is increasing day by day. He wants to be number one at any stage but slips down and fear of failure keeps on mounting up with every incident.

The research work available on bullying suggests that a bully who tends to show himself as a very strong person is actually a very weak and fragile character suffering from mental illness. Researches suggest that he needs sympathy and acceptance of the people. In fact, he has been bullied by someone or the situation in which he is living has developed a negative approach and feelings. Whatever he is doing, actually he is trying to overcome his own weakness and through bullying any weak person he gets satisfaction and pleasure as he thinks that he is taking revenge. These are symptoms of mental illness and the boy mentioned here is in the same situation.

It is not the universal truth that only children and the people who are not able to achieve prestigious positions are at the receiving end of the above mentioned fate, it can happen with anyone. I am mentioning the third case study in this regard. This is the case of a gazetted officer. No doubt, this post is held by an educated person. I mean to say that only education is not sufficient in eradicating the presence of fear. It needs sanity, the ultimate satisfaction which is hardly possible for human beings. The officer was enjoying life in his own way. He had a habit of self- praise and wanted to be at the pole position in the office which was not possible in the presence of senior officers. He enjoyed his luck at times but when he had to face the real situation, it was tough for him to accept the truth. Though he pretended to show that he was very happy, his facial expression and activities were witnessing the real story which was going through in his mind.

With each passing day, his mental status could not bear the fear of losing his pole position to another officer in the same office and in front of the officials whose he had been head of office and was proud of it. He felt humiliated while everything whatever was going on was exactly right and he was getting his actual dues but he was over ambitious and was not satisfied. This case is about not accepting the truth. He was a junior officer and officials were still respecting him but he was afraid that in the presence of the senior officer who was the head of office, he might not be able to enjoy the previous position. The fear of losing respect which he desperately needed led him into depression.

At the initial stage, the staff members could not understand his reality. As soon as the new officer joined the office, he started saying that he is feeling very much relieved and happy. The staff members thought that it could be true as workload for any person could put him under tremendous pressure and it gives pleasure when someone else takes over the charge. But, when he repeatedly began to utter the same feelings, staff members realized that whatever he is expressing is not exactly true. Actually, he is trying to hide his nervousness and in this process wants to pose himself as cool and calm. It is a fact that whenever people see someone hiding the truth for no real and genuine reason, they tend to ignore it and take it as a part and parcel of life. So, in this case the staff members did not care much and became busy with their own duties which was compulsory.

As the time progressed, his statements fumbled. He used to praise his senior officer in front of him but did not hesitate to tell a lot of bad things about the senior officer in his absence. Though he had surrendered against his officer due to fear, his efforts were on to regain his position. Actually, with each mishap, the doubts were being pointed towards him though it might be the mischieves of others. He used to clarify his position before asking him so everyone looked at him suspecting. All these happenings which should be very normal and it is seen in the offices everywhere as people take it easy as it is their duty but he could not take it easy due to his own weakness. Actually, before the senior officers joined, he used to say that someday his position will be changed and it was this fear which always crept in his mind. As he could not tolerate this situation because of his own created misconception that his social reputation was in danger and it led to a lot of problems for him later on he slipped into depression.

Case study four, This is a case of a student who was preparing for competitive exams after completing his post graduation. He was a good student and used to devote a lot of time to his studies. His aim was to crack competitive exams and get a reputed administrative job. Whenever I saw him, he was busy studying. He was determined to fulfill his desire and he sacrificed everything in order to succeed. He thought that through continuous study of syllabus, competitive exams can be passed. He did not bother to think about holistic development. The concept of personality development was useless for him. Just reading the books was enough.

Now, the time had come to test his ability and hard work. The competitive exams are a different ball game. These are far from the routine standard passing exams. A student's ability and hard work is measured with the performances of other competitors. So, no one can be assured. A student can give his best but he can do nothing if the others are performing better than him. He started to apply for various competitive exams and began to appear in each exam. After many unsuccessful attempts, his patience broke down. He began to doubt his own ability and knowledge. Though his efforts continued, the results were the same. He was hopeless. Actually, he was working very hard so there was no sign of carelessness. He was in a dilemma.

Meanwhile, his contemporary students whom he considered weaker than him, were getting success one by one. Then a heart broken incident happened. Two of his juniors who had just started to appear in such exams, got selected in the same exam in which he also had appeared. This time his problem was more severe. It was not due to his own unsuccessful attempt as he was becoming habitual of such things, it was due to the success of his two juniors which he could not tolerate and there was a drastic change in his behaviour. He became very introverted and avoided facing others. If anyone tried to console him, he showed abrupt behaviour. It was a mental shock for him and he had to take medicine and still he is not fully recovered though he is earning well to look after his family.

The above mentioned case is very sad and misfortunate for anybody. With the help of career counselling, such things can be avoided but he could not get the counselling services when he needed the most. The student was working very hard throughout his attempts and was quite confident of achieving his target. But he could not. Why? The reason is that he did not analyze the situation. It was a lack of awareness. He purchased the required books of well known authors and started studying. As we know that in competitive exams, the posts are limited and candidates are selected as per the merit list which is prepared after exams. So, it does not give anyone guarantee to get through. He judged only his potential and ability and was not enough to judge others and the demands of the situation.

At the initial stage of the competitive exams, after not getting success, he took it as normal. He thought that in the coming attempt he would succeed but his confidence became very low after a series of unsuccessful attempts. Now, there was a fear of failure always present with him. He started thinking that he might not get through. He felt ashamed as others were cracking the exams whom he considered inferior to him. It was very tough to get selected in competitive exams with such a low confidence as he had. He was struggling to regroup himself but a sequence of his failures and others' success left a scare on his mind and gradually he became mentally upset.

Such cases are a never- ending process. We often come across such incidents in our society. Generally, people do not want to understand the mindset of such people. They think that the sufferers are usually narrow- minded and do not easily mix up with others. Some fears such as darkness, ghosts, insecurity, etc. which often appear deadly but as we grow old, we are able to overcome them so their effects are not permanent. Fear of social rejection and fear of failure are the most prominent which are very harmful and leave a never- healing impact sometimes.

Actually, fears are like an illusion. As much as people think of it, they are able to grasp the positivity of people and spread negativity. People begin to think about the negative aspects and slowly and slowly it becomes their habit. As every individual is a part of society so his/ her abnormal behaviour becomes disgusting for others and is often neglected by others. It affects his mind and sometimes consequences are very hazardous which is explained in the next chapter.

THE FINGERPRINTS OF FEAR–AN ANALYTICAL APPROACH

The stories of childhood not only provide pleasure when we are grown up but also open the door for learning. The purpose of sharing the stories is to enhance the knowledge in an interesting way so that the audience might be able to grasp it. When we start thinking on a particular topic in a broad perspective, our vision becomes more transparent and clear and we are able to understand in a comprehensive way. Once during a family gathering, I came to know about such a narrative which justifies that fear always leaves its fingerprints.

This story belongs to a wood cutter who used to go into the forest to bring wood. It was his profession and he was earning his livelihood through it for many years. One day he became very late as he wanted to collect more wood and in this process it became dark. Though he was habitual of such situations yet he wanted to come back as fast as he could. He collected all the wood and tied it with a rope and came back. He was very tired so after reaching home, he kept the bundle of wood outside the house and went in. He had dinner and fell asleep. In the morning, as he was still in the bed, he heard the fearful voice of his wife. Guessing his wife was in trouble he at once rushed towards the outside and found his wife screaming and pointing out towards the bundle of wood. He could not understand what was going on so he asked his wife, "why are you screaming?" Now, somehow restoring her breath she said, "why did you do so?" He again asked, "what have I done?" Pointing out towards the bundle she said, "see at bundle. You have tied the bundle with a snake." As soon as he saw the bundle tied with a snake he was shocked. He shivered with fear. He could not believe that he had done so. He immediately looked at himself in search of finding out the mark of snake sting as it was a probability. Though he could not find the proof of the sting in spite of checking minutely, from the very moment he believed that he would be affected sooner or later. In this process, his fear went on increasing with the course of time. He frequently visited doctors in this regard and it took several months when anyhow he managed to cope up with his existing fear.

This incident might look very common to someone but it was very painful for the concerned person. He had to waste his lot of time and money in overcoming his fear. When we are caught in such situations, we experience reality and there is no way to escape but when we come out of such incidents and narrate it to others, sometimes people take it very lightly and enjoy it. We see that the person was very normal and did not show any symptom of fear till he came to know about the incident. But, as soon as he became familiar with his act, his mindset changed at once. He did not bother to think that if anything was wrong with him, it could be felt. He was thinking that something dangerous might happen in future and that was the real issue of fear. After some months, he realized that everything was OK but till then he wasted a lot of time and money.

It is true that everybody fears though it might be momentary in some cases. When we see the danger spontaneously and become afraid, this situation exists till it passes and the situation becomes normal then we feel safe ourselves. Such situations occur due to natural processes so our fear vanishes with time. In such cases when we assume that it might happen again and is related to social issues though it is hypothetical yet, it is very harmful. As we know, human behaviour is very strange. It is due to the fear which exists in people's minds in conceptual form which forces them to behave in a specific way and whatever they do, it is always to justify them right before society. But the truth is, they do it because of fear. I am mentioning an instance here in this regard.

If you look back into the socio-economic system forty or forty five years ago, you will find a totally different scenario in comparison to the present one. The financial status of the people was not up to the mark so due to lack of money they were deprived of many things but they seldom complained. They were content, usually believing that it was their bad luck so no need to panic. Generally, the eldest son of the family used to get all the facilities that family had. It was often seen that he was supported in all respects to get education and others had to wait. It is human nature that he always wants to get more and more. The members of a family who were fortunate to get all the facilities and respect from others desperately wanted to maintain their position at any cost and the thought of losing their superior position always used to give discomfort to them and that was the origin of fear.

It is the case of a person who was a member of a joint family. He was pampered by each member as he was the eldest son of the family. He was continuously getting the affection and respect of the family members in all aspects. It was the time when children were not pressurized for studies. Only promoting the class without getting failed in the same class was considered a good achievement. Generally, students used to give up studies after two or more years repeating the same class and especially in class tenth board exams so even passing the exam after scoring more than forty five percent marks was regarded as a good one. He was fulfilling the requirements of parents and completed his education. He got married and settled with his family. The respect from the family and society continued. We know that life is not as simple as we want to live. Any situation is certain to change with the course of time. As soon as the people get older, their priority changes and so their mindset diverges in other domains which are more important.

The other family members also began to lead life independently. People don't have control over the happenings of their life. They have to accept it. In this case, the most noteworthy issue was that the person's wife was illiterate. It was very common during that period but the other female members of the family were far superior and the problem started here. It was not an issue for any family members as they were busy with their own work but it created a doubt in the person's mind. He thought that his wife might not be able to get the same position in the family which he was acquiring. Slowly and slowly the doubt turned into fear. Though nobody ever showed disrespect towards his wife, his concept was always with him.

In this regard, whenever he got a chance, he never hesitated to insult other members to show his superiority. Initially family members could not understand the reason behind his frustration but they tried to escape themselves from his outburst. His abrupt behaviour did not change so he began to lose real respect from others. Though people accompanied him as per his requirement but the healthy environment was always absent in his presence due to lack of trust. He did not realize that his act was breaking his relationships as the fear of losing respect for family was always there though hypothetical.

We can easily find such incidents in the family and society. Actually, the people who are getting pole position in the family for a long time always wishes to maintain it not only for themselves but for their wives and children also. They become very passionate regarding their status in the family and want to keep it up by hook or crook. They forget that it is not their birthright. Everybody needs respect from the family and society and he earns it through his good manners and giving his vital support to family and society when someone is in need. The problem lies with the person who wants it as a heredity and in this process his fear compelled him to do unsocial activities which turns harmful for him and his family.

In some cases, fear in psychological form always follows and people tend to live in tension despite positive happenings in their life. They don't see the bright aspect of their lives, instead they look at the dark side due to their negative mindset which is because of their existing fear. The present case is the true testimony of such people. It is a self reflection of a cancer patient. Once he was present in a motivational session organized for cancer patients to empower and enable them to realize that the battle of such life threatening disease can be won. It is a proven fact that it requires sheer determination and a positive approach to be a winner. Low confidence is the key factor in depriving people from leading a happy life.

Before expressing his feelings, it is vital to mention his case history of existing disease. The person has been in the clutches of cancer for the past ten years. He has successfully negotiated it through proper treatment and blessings of almighty and his age is seventy plus. After the end of the motivational session, he said in his feedback that the battle of cancer cannot be won. You have to live with it. His tension was easily visible on his face and voice. He was the oldest patient in the group and the most fortunate one to survive for so long from such a dangerous disease.

Now, it is very necessary to analyze the impact of his statement ' The battle cannot be won'. I do not believe that ninety nine out of hundred people find it very strange keeping in mind the period he has survived and looking at his present age. But, first of all try to see from his own perspective. Though he has almost seen the world as a human being yet the desire is there to carry on as no one wants to depart from this world till a little hope exists. The love and affection of family members prohibits them from doing so. The second factor compelled us a lot to think about in this case.

Imagine the situation when the family members come to know about the cancer, they are stunned. If the condition of family members is so terrible, we can easily imagine the mindset of the patient. How can we expect him to have a positive approach? But, time is a great healer and we know as the time progresses, the intensity of pain reduces. It is a fact which we encounter in our day to day life that life is at risk everywhere. There is no guarantee for anyone to live for a certain time. Surviving so long from cancer is like a miracle. I find it the blessings of God. As the person thinks that the battle from cancer cannot be won but most of us will definitely agree that he successfully faced and overcame it.

The question is- 'Why is he thinking so?' The answer is quite plain and simple. He is very much attached with his family and doesn't want to separate from his family due to the disease at any cost. Everybody knows that cancer is very dangerous, so it has mounted tremendous tension on him and he is living in tension. Though a long time has passed in which he has been fortunate to survive but because of enormous tension which is increasing always, he is not able to realize that he is winning the battle each day and his such long survival can bring hope to another patient that they can survive too for such a long period. The fear of losing his life has created tension and it is the reason behind his negative mindset otherwise he should thank God and his family and be content. Sometimes fear does not allow people to celebrate whatever they have achieved.

Fear comes in so many diversified forms that sometimes it is tough to believe but the truth needs no verification. This case is related to fear of corporal punishment by a parent in which academic career of the concerned child was hardly saved. This is the case of a class six student who used to be a good student but the expectation from the parent was very high which he was unable to fulfill so he started hiding the truth. The fear of corporal punishment was such that he had to pay heavily for it and became victim of doing unsocial activity which could be avoided easily in a healthy parental relationship.

It is common in the schools that few students take responsibility for depositing their fee. Sometimes in the absence of class teachers or any other reason they have to wait for the next day so they have to keep the fee themselves and deposit it when the class teacher is available. It looks like a very common process but sometimes it creates problems. It happens when the students spend their money without the permission of their parents and in some cases where the parent's behaviour is very strict, they often don't inform the parents and try to manage on their own. The same situation happened with the student mentioned here. He spent his school fee and did not inform the parents. His name struck off and he became terrified. The question was- how to disclose the matter to the parent? With each passing day his fear went on mounting. As it was the time in which students prepare for the exam at home and become irregular so he got a chance to stay back to prepare for the exams. The examination was over and he was unable to appear in the exams but he used to leave the home as per schedule of exams so that nobody could guess. After the declaration of result anyhow he managed to escape by assuring his parents that he had passed with good marks. As his father used to force him to study always, he purchased the books for the next class and ordered him to start studying.

After reopening the school in the next session he again started as usual. In the beginning of the session, he started to pretend not going to school and this created doubt. His cousin could not believe whatever he told so he decided to look into the matter. His cousin was an ex- student of the same school and was familiar with the teachers. He asked the name of his class teacher and met him to verify what was actually going on. He was shocked to know the whole matter. He found that the boy was not enrolled in the class which he had told, instead he was in the same class as his name was struck- off due to non- payment of fee.

The boy was very much terrified and began to request his cousin not disclose the matter to his father as the consequence could be dangerous for him. His cousin somehow managed the situation and his academic journey which was in jeopardy, again started. Such situations might be more which are unable to come in limelight and the career of many students have been ruined because of fear of corporal punishment of the parents. Such incidents tell itself the story of fear which hampers the interpersonal relations among family members and they have to pay the price for it.

While analyzing the case, it can be understood that this situation could be easily averted. Not only the boy but the family members were also suffering as social humiliation was there for everybody. In society, people enjoy narrating such incidents and don't sympathize. They are unable to understand the trauma of the victim. He was in constant fear for four or five months. It looks horrifying while even imagining. Actually, the concept of fear once created, is very hard to overpower and the same happened with the boy. He never thought to explain the matter to his father. Had he ever managed to tell, definitely the situation would be smooth but he could not.

Now, the incident which I am mentioning here reflects the fear of failure which I came across during the senior secondary board exam. We often find the parents accompanying their wards at the exams. Maybe, some parents come as it is necessary to leave their wards as they are unable to reach due to lack of public transport and some come willingly to protect and support their wards. I noticed a student who was surrounded by his parents and brother. His mother was holding his hand and was looking very nervous, so was his father. His mother accompanied him to the entry gate and was looking anxiously at him even after her son was out of her sight.

The most important thing in this incident was that the student was looking very relaxed. It might be as he was quite aware of his preparation so he was full of confidence. It might be that he would have been a proven good student and had full faith in his ability. Here, the parents are feeling the heat. They might have their own expectations and that had prompted them to feel pressure. As we know, till the outcome of the result, everything is hidden. Even the slightest assumption of failure creates fear. People tend to feel nervousness not because of themselves only but also for their dear ones. When the hopes are very high, the agony of fulfilling the task mounts pressure.

In such cases, the nervousness of the parents becomes a drawback for the children. Actually, parents are creating so much pressure on themselves as well as their wards that it affects the performance of the children. Parents are unable to realize that their unlimited love and affection is becoming a barrier as they are always discussing the future of their wards as per their liking. Children are unable to enjoy their lives because the environment of the family rarely allows them to do so. A very handful are able to perform as per their ability by coping up the pressure while most of them find it difficult.

We often witness the incident of students committing suicide. Recently I came through a news that a student committed suicide due to poor performance in the exams. Such incidents are very terrifying. Families are unable to cope up with such situations. Success and failure are the part and parcel of life. Such things are not only for a single individual, it is for everybody, so there is no need to panic. Life is there to face the challenges and come as a winner. It is the moral duty of family, society and nation to take firm and appropriate steps to avoid such mishappenings. After such incidents, the families suffer a lot. The scar remains forever.

Above mentioned few situations are mere reflection of whatever is happening in the realm of fear. We can see the victims of tension, anxiety, nervousness, depression, suicide, failure, low confidence and negativity everywhere. Everyone wants to be a key member of the society and nation to stamp his superiority. In this process, they are creating a lot of pressure on themselves. The fear of lagging behind others causes fear which sometimes becomes disastrous and the concerned person has to feel the pain throughout life.

The question is- "Are we compelled to live in fear?" The answer cannot be given in a word as every situation can be changed but it requires dedicated efforts. It needs to see things in a holistic perspective. Everything is possible if we adopt a realistic approach. Healthy competition opens the door of personal development and creates new milestones. Always remember don't try to be like others but be yourself because you are too good.

CHANNELIZATION OF FEAR:– THE NEED OF HOUR

Friends, it is necessary to see things from different perspectives as it unfolds our vision. When I find people reacting differently to a stimulus situation, my curiosity increases. In this regard, I often try to find out the factors and elements behind it. As per my interaction with people in search of finding out the reason, I feel that channelizing the thought process plays a vital role in coping with the situation. It mainly depends on positive and negative aspects of people so in this way, their concepts are decisive factors. It is rightly said that if you want your life to be better, shift your thoughts and feelings to a better place and the universe will match it. There is so much ease and abundance waiting for you in the place of feeling good but you have to step into the place of feeling good to have it all.

In our day to day life, we face many situations which affect our thinking, feelings and actions. It is often seen that sometimes we are rewarded without putting much effort into our work while sometimes our best efforts are ignored. We cannot take it easy when we are at the receiving end. When we feel happy or hurt our reactions dictate the proceedings of our life at the moment. If such situations are happening consistently then our reactions be it positive or negative and later on becomes our habit. It affects our each activity and it reflects on our performance. I mean to say that it happens when we cannot control the happenings as per our ability. It is often seen that sometimes we are held responsible for the failure which is actually determined on the basis of a wrong judgment. Now, in this regard I am mentioning here a story which can provide a better picture to see things in a positive perspective, so that we could survive ourselves from negativity which comes due to wrong judgment and no one can be held responsible as it can only be considered the stroke of destiny.

This is a story of two friends who were very good artists. They were living together happily. The ruling king of the kingdom was a good admirer of painting so he wished to have a painter who was the best to appoint him as his court painter. He called the painters in this regard. Among the painters, these two friends were shortlisted. They were equally good so the king could not decide on which one to appoint so he decided to take a test and on the basis of the test the painter was going to be selected for the position of court painter. The venue was decided. In a big hall, both were told to make a painting on the wall and the hall was divided by a curtain. They were given a period of one month to complete their assignment.

The situation was tricky because there was only one post and both of them wanted to get this prestigious post so they decided to give their best. As both were not allowed to discuss or see each other's painting due to tests so both concentrated on their work. Everyone has his own way of expressing his talent and ability. One of them immediately decided his project and started to work to complete it in its best form within the stipulated time while the other was not totally satisfied with whatever he used to do so after doing a bit, he used to think he was able to make better whatever he had made and used to rub it off. Then again he used to start his work. Both were busy in their own work in their own way.

After completion of stipulated time, now, it was the turn of judgment. The king came with his ministers to see the paintings. When he saw the painting of the first painter, he was quite impressed and remarked it was 'the best'. He said to his ministers that it was the best painting so no need to see the painting of the other painter as no one could make it better than this one. His ministers requested him to see the painting of another painter before arriving at the final result as it was necessary to see other's painting for the transparency in the result. The king agreed and he pulled the curtain which was dividing the hall.

When the king saw the painting of the other painter, he was astonished to see the artistry of the painter. It seemed that he had made the painting inside the wall. He was so impressed that he at once announced his winner and ordered the minister to appoint him and went away.

Now, my friends, you will be thinking that it is an example of simple judgement. The king declared the painter the winner who had made the better painting. But, do you know, the winner had not made the painting? I know, you will easily not believe but it is true. There will be wandering a lot of questions in your mind and should be. Actually what happened??

The first painter as I have mentioned earlier started his work and completed it within stipulated time. The other painter could not make the painting as he used to rub after making some part of it. An interesting thing happened during this process. While rubbing the wall frequently it became like a mirror as the wall was made of stone and as soon as the king pulled the curtain, the painting by the first painter reflected on the wall. Actually whatever the king saw was a mere reflection of the painting of the first one and the king could not understand the reason. He gave his judgement whatever he saw. We can't simply blame the king for his mistake, it was not intentionally done. But, the question still stands. How did he make the wrong judgement? The story ends here as each story has to come to an end at some points but life does not. Such happenings are still frequently occuring and we are witnessing. Now, try to see and analyze different types of reactions in such situations.

It is a human tendency that if people are deprived of their genuine right, they will not tolerate it easily. Their hearts might be broken in some cases as they are unable to bear injustice. They might think it as their misfortune and get depressed. They might fight against the system and in this process, they will have to use their time, energy and resources which they can utilize in other things. They might take it as part and parcel of life. Though frustration, anger are sure to follow in such situations, the way people react in such situations counts very much as it directs and controls their future.

Actually, we can't totally stop the flow of emotions and feelings which come out as the reaction of happenings of our day to day life. Sometimes these feelings play havoc as people are unable to control their feelings and their responses are very disgraceful and harmful not only for them but for others also. It is rightly said that an emotional mind never allows the people to make correct decisions in their life. But decisions taken with cool minds lead people to achieve their dreams.

It is my personal experience that as human beings, we are not the controller of our destiny. In our day to day life, we find that there are so many things which are happening in our life beyond our wishes which can be made better if we do accordingly. So, whatever we can do, we should try to do our best. It is a proven fact that each individual wishes to lead a happy and peaceful life and wants to keep himself/ herself far from tension, anxiety and stress. The question is- Is it really possible? Perhaps- No. There are valid reasons to prove. As we know that if we want to reach the highest level, we will have to put in a lot of effort. Bigger achievements bring bigger challenges which we have to face. The aspirants can't run away from these challenges if they want to taste success and in this process, stress is bound to occur. We can find stress everywhere, at home, in an educational institution, at work places or in a social set up. It is difficult to ignore it and it tends to destabilize a person's life in all domains i.e. physically, mentally, psychologically and emotionally.

Actually, past experiences play a vital role in creating fear which generates pressure. It is human tendency that whatever he has experienced in the past or the experiences shared by others often come to mind at the crucial juncture of life. It is often seen that before starting an important work or appearing in the exams, everyone feels pressure. Each individual handles the situation in his own way. It is the demand of the situation and his ability to face the challenges determine the intensity of the pressure. The fear of failure puts enormous stress which is necessary to release.

From childhood onwards, most people develop the habit of getting each and everything whatever they wish. The situations where they are unable to get their desired result become very painful for them to accept. We often see in our day to day life that in some families, they pamper their wards a lot. Always try to support and protect them as much as they can. They don't give their wards a chance to see things in their own way. As we know, life is a learning process. Everybody faces sweet and sour moments and these are valuable lessons which are very helpful for the future.

Generally, a lot of valuable time goes in vain. We think so much and tension surrounds us. There are many factors for not achieving desired success. It cannot be regarded as a fault. Each individual's capabilities are not equal. Someone can achieve it in a short period through his/ her inborn qualities whereas someone has to spend more time. Failure only means that it needs more effort from you, it does not mean that you are not good enough. Motivation and inspiration are the key factors in getting success.

If you carefully see ants doing their work, you will find that they have to do the same things repeatedly to complete it. It is because of their small physical structure which demands more effort from them to accomplish their work. The most important fact is that they are never tired in completing their task. They do successfully because of their will power. Always think that God has provided us enormous capabilities and if we are unable to perform as per our capabilities then there is no need to repent. Continuous efforts never go useless. Our job is to reduce the pressure which has mounted due to our negativity. No need to panic, just keep your efforts on.

As we are identified as social creatures, we are certain to live with other people most of the time in our lives. The persons with whom we have to frequently interact are- family members, friends, neighbours, relatives and the people at our workplaces. There are a lot of variations among people in terms of life styles, social status and financial status which can be seen easily everywhere. When someone compares himself/ herself with others, he finds these differences which sometimes become a cause of concern for him. He finds it really hard to accept it as the intensity of dissatisfaction continuously increases.

It is a general human tendency that when he gets to know that he is on the superior side, he experiences a sense of satisfaction and happiness and life looks beautiful. On the other hand, when he regards himself inferior in comparison to others, he tries to fill this gap and puts efforts to overtake them and, in this way, pressure mounts up. Comparing ourselves with others can be helpful in a healthy competitive environment. An individual definitely tries to uplift his/ her performance when he/ she observes that it is essential to reach a particular level. Everybody wants to be successful and in this process tries to give his best.

The world is full of wonderful inventions and researches of human beings in almost every field which might once considered impossible to do so. We can't actually imagine what is going to happen in the future but when such things happen, it provides name, fame and money to the concerned person and people idolize him/ her. Taking inspiration from such things helps a lot but we don't need to think about repeating or surpassing their performances. If we engage ourselves in such things then we can't develop divergent thinking which is quite necessary for showing our potential and ability in our own way. There are so many variations among us in physical, mental and emotional domains which affect our performances and reflect in our personal development and achievements.

Our main purpose must be based on analyzing our strength and weakness and enabling and empower ourselves to bring out inherent potential and perform as per our capabilities. The focus should be on the maximum utilization of available resources. The problems begin when we don't listen to our hearts. We just ignore our inner voice and follow what others expect from us due to social or family pressure. It causes stress and troubles and we feel helpless and hopeless. You are the best judge of yourself. You know better about your potential and capabilities so never regret failures, just stand up and move ahead. Always believe that new avenues are awaiting for you to show your potential.

Now, here is an interesting question- If someone is not able to get desired success then who is to be blamed- he, ownself or destiny?. First of all, we ask ourselves questions about our performances and it becomes very tricky in the case of failures. The questions are certainly to follow, we cannot avoid these questions. As much as we try to ignore, it comes with double force so it is better to search the answers rather than just avoiding. There are two situations of failure. In the first one, the concerned people take it lightly. They don't bother to think seriously even for a moment. Only see their outcomes and their focus shift whatever they are doing. You may find it a bit strange. Why do they react in such a quiet manner? Their reaction is based on their pre- concept. They are quite aware of whatever they have done earlier. They know that they don't need to panic as they are totally dependent on destiny so in case of getting success, they would have considered themselves fortunate. In the case of failure, they don't want to cry as they don't take it as a personal failure. The most interesting reason behind their satisfaction is that there are more people standing with them as failures and some of them have put in more effort than them. It gives them a sense of contentment and pleasure and they don't regret not doing sincere efforts and are still hopeful that with the stroke of luck they will get desired success.

On the other hand, we find a totally different scenario.

This category consists of the people who have done each and everything whatever was in their stride to achieve success but still success eluded them. Dejection is sure to follow in such cases as they are also called 'the victims of destiny.' I have given

the term due to valid reasons, our destiny follows us everywhere we go. It is not only related

to outcomes only but it is also related to the facilities we get during the course of time. In the present time of fierce competition, facilities play a key role in getting success. How can a soldier fight with others without proper and equivalent effective weapons? During the school days, it does not affect the performance much but as the time progresses, its importance increases.

We often see in our family, neighbourhood and society that many aspirants of engineering, medical, civil services, higher post in defence are honestly doing their job to get success. But, when we look at the facilities they are getting for preparation, the variations are so much. These variations are the difference between success and failure in most of the cases. Now, how can we blame him for his failure? He did whatever he could. But, the question is here to console. Can he console himself on the basis that he could achieve success as he was short of required facilities. Surely, he will not, because he was quite sure of his success as he had worked hard. So, in such cases, a proper effort from a family member is necessary to make him feel that he is not responsible for failure and sooner or later his/ her hard work will pay off.

It is a strange human behaviour that people start thinking about the outcome before the beginning of exams or assigned work. This habit puts enormous pressure on them. There are many factors which become activated in actual situations which generally we can't think about during planning. It is a general tendency that whenever we are well prepared for any specific test exam or work, our confidence gives us belief in setting desired results. It inspires us for good performance as our confidence level is very high. In this process, people often forget that there are a large number of candidates who have equally prepared like him. The main factor is execution. Whatever they have prepared, it is very important to execute that preparation accordingly to achieve success.

When people are focusing so much on the outcome of their exams before appearing, it can be harmful for them. As much as they think, concentration will get diverted and it can hamper their final preparation. Sometimes thinking repeatedly about the outcome creates doubt in getting success. It is connected to our thought process. When we think so much on a particular topic positive and negative thoughts are sure to follow. Whenever someone realizes that there are so many candidates so the result might not be as per expectation, he becomes very nervous and it causes harmful outcomes.

So, whatever you are going to do, concentrate fully on completing the task. Try to save yourself from losing your focus. Maintain your willpower and motivation. Always be positive and believe that consistent efforts always reward. Ensure that you are working hard as per your ability and potential. Think that you are doing your task honestly and are committed to give your best. Realize that it is in your hand to give your best but you can't stop others who can put in more effort than you. Just wait and see what is restored in your future.

As we know, life is not an easy going process. Interruptions come in life to test the ability of each individual. Problems are part and parcel of our day to day life which we have to face at any cost. The frequency of problems may be more or less for each person but it is certain that problems will come for everyone. The notion of the problems can't be defined exactly as these are the situations which an individual finds difficult to cope up with. Any given problem can be tough for someone to face and on the other hand can be a smooth sailing for others.

The horizon of problems is very vast which starts from childhood and continuously moves on throughout entire life. The starting few years of life are an easy ride in which almost each individual gets a chance to spend in the midst of love and affection of parents and other family members. As soon as a child enters the school for academic excellence, he sees an entirely new environment in comparison to a family where he is bound to adjust himself to survive and learn. He meets the children who have come from different socio- economic backgrounds. Some children easily adapt to the school environment while some others find it difficult to adjust. Previous experience helps in this regard. The children who have spent time in pre- nursery schools easily mix- up while the freshers take time.

Actually, the problems of school time are solved with the help of teachers, parents and peers. The helping hands are always there to lift up in need. When students reach senior secondary level, they are expected to guide themselves. They have to make decisions particularly in the academic field. Any wrong decision can be a drawback for their future. Their choice of streams, getting admission in a reputed institution, financial support, etc. determine their future. After completing the education, they step into the world of competitions. Even the toppers of schools and colleges here find different scenarios. There is a level of each competitive exam which requires specific preparation and the standard of candidates are quite good. So, the chance of getting selected cannot be guaranteed. After marriage the responsibility increases and it requires a balance. It often causes trouble if someone is unable to shoulder the responsibility. Problems also occur at the workplace as people have to work with others whose behaviour is quite different. So, all the problems are part of life and bound to happen sooner or later.

It is seen that people often break down while coping up with problems. They as well as their family suffer heavily. These problems are not only for a set of people in society but for the mass. We have to be physically, mentally and emotionally strong to face the challenges thrown at us. People have their own perception in facing the problem of day to day life. What actually happens is that someone panics at the sight of the crisis and they start cursing their own fortunes in this regard and don't try to face the crisis situation. Some problems can be negotiated by putting a bit of extra effort.

It is human behaviour that when he finds himself in trouble , most of the time he gets irritated. He thinks that he is alone who is facing such problems while others are enjoying themselves. Such negative thinking is painful. If we try to see things from a broad perspective, we will find that there are other people who are surrounded even in the bigger problems. It takes time to overcome the problems. Patience is very important in this situation as it provides a healthy environment to think properly and positively. Realize that you are quite capable of solving the problems and if you will surpass this test, you will get a lot in return. The most important point is that problems are there to be solved. These occur for a time being only. So, be positive and move ahead. Try to channelize your fear to get rid of negative thinking and you will be able to see the rainbow of happiness.

BELIEVE IN YOURSELF – EXPLORE YOUR POTENTIAL

It is rightly said that a small dot can stop a big sentence but a few more dots can give it continuity. Amazing but true. Every ending initiates a new beginning. That's life.

There are some questions which need to be unfolded to facilitate us in our life at crucial juncture.

Who prompts us to get angry and frustrated?

The adverse situations of our life.

Why are we controlled by situations?

Due to inadaptability with the situations.

Who is more blessed- person or situation?

Definitely the person.

Why do people generally surrender to situations?

It is due to lack of will power to face the crisis.

How can people develop the required will power?

Certainly from themselves.

How?

By empowering themselves, by bringing out their inherent potential.

Why do people tend to ignore their potential?

Lack of self- awareness and lack of positive attitude are the key factors in this regard.

As we are quite aware, when destiny smiles on us, we assume life as a bed of roses but it changes into a double edged sword when the rays of fortune disappear. It is a well known fact that a majority of people are unable to utilize their maximum potentials due to lack of awareness, tension, timely support and proper guidance. It is a proven reality that each individual needs help and support to face stress, trauma and anxiety. In this situation counselling is required to reduce tension and make life meaningful.

We are constantly witnessing the increasing problems of unemployment, violence, crimes, suicides and substance abuse such as drugs and alcohol and so on. The main reason behind this is the socio- economic structures of the society in which people are unable to cope up the stress due to lack of guidance and counselling.

It is quite obvious that every individual needs help throughout his/ her lifespan to get essential information, advice and directions which play a vital role in achieving desired results. It is the combined responsibility of family, school and society to ensure that each individual could get this facility. Particularly school which is regarded as the best place where the personality of a child develops at its best.

Guidance is based on the assumption that human beings have inherent potential for development. Their capabilities can be utilized by providing them the right experience and insight into their own problems. The role of educational institutions and teachers has become very important. Teachers can lay the foundation for developing the skills in the children to take right decisions. Guidance involves not only

understanding the students but also the social surroundings of the students.

It has to be imparted in the context of holistic development of personality in which children could realize their potential after getting proper assistance and support at each stage of life. It helps them in analyzing the past and learning from the previous experiences to prevent wasting energies which can go in vain in regretting previous discontentment and frustrations. It channelizes the strength to adapt changes in behaviour to live more effectively and perform as per their true potentials.

Guidance is not only a one to one interaction but it is also available for students having common needs in various areas of personal and social life, educational and career pursuits which would help in proper utilization of manpower. The strength of a nation consists in its citizens. If the children are well equipped with resources, they would be able to remove evils from the society which would be helpful in achieving individual and national goals.

An individual's own problem gradually becomes the problem of society as we see the increasing problems of the children addicted to drugs and alcohols, a large number of abused children, cases of suicides, gender bias, violence, school dropouts, unemployment and bankruptcy of values spreading all over the world. These problems require remedial treatment as well as preventive efforts of the guidance profession. Awareness programme for students and community groups should be organized.

Guidance and counselling is required for various purposes. It is not only related to educational achievements but also extends to mental health, interpersonal relations, career development and work adjustment. It is directed to promote the holistic development of each individual.

Educational growth helps in developing the abilities and skills for life-long learning, identifying the difficulties in subject matter & learning process in overcoming the problems developing healthy and positive attitude, habit and moral values towards work through awareness of the world of work, planning and preparation of one's career. It develops social skills and a positive approach for leading a happy and contented personal- social life.

It provides help regarding difficulties in academics and adjustment to the environment, informs about the educational alternatives available to them and enables them to realize and understand the relation between educational and occupational choices. Most of the parents and students are not aware about the various contemporary courses and career options. They need help in this regard which can be fulfilled through guidance & counselling. It promotes the culture of work ethics and dignity of labour and enables them to learn more about themselves and the world of work to make choices and plans.

It assists in leading a good family life to an individual who can transform the family environment into a healthy and pleasing one. Develop the right attitudes and values, co-operation and tolerance. All these are helpful in promoting unity and national integration. Thus, they can channelize their energy for the betterment of society and nation. There are various physical and social- emotional developments which take place in each stage of life so it is important to understand these developments. It helps in understanding the pressure and tension which are barriers in personal development and adjustment.

The aim of guidance & counselling is to recognize and realize the potentials of children and nourish these potentials. It focuses on a holistic approach which takes into account the individual potential as well as outside socio- cultural factors which affect the individuals. As we know that there are some stages in a person's life particularly during adolescence which are crucial for development and adjustment. The realization of the potential depends on environmental assistance which consists of removal of blocks which are acting as barriers in healthy growth.

We find a wide range of individual differences among people. It is because each individual has a unique combination of characteristics which provide uniqueness to each person. This understanding is at the heart of the guidance programme. Guidance provided by a professional serves as the catalyst for the expression of these individual differences. Identification of individual freedom, worth, respect and dignity is the hallmark of guidance. It helps an individual to explore his/ her ability and potential.

Guidance is considered as an integral part of school education for the holistic development of the personality of the students. Guidance and learning are very much related to each other. There is so much pressure on students for academic achievement. The cause of concern is that they want to get it at the expense of overall development. It is vital to look out for factors which influence learning and help students to achieve to their maximum.

The guidance programme helps the students by finding out the reasons for under- achievement and makes efforts to help the children understand the difficulties and problems faced and facilitate them for better performance. Guidance personnel provide an opportunity to students to understand their potentials and abilities, needs and aspirations so that they can use it at maximum and do not get upset by their shortcomings.

We see that a healthy and unhealthy environment at home plays a major role in learning. Whereas a healthy environment provides all kinds of support to evolve, the children from unhealthy environments find it difficult to concentrate on study as the sour memories follow them everywhere. This may be harmful for their mental & emotional well-being. Generally, such children are unable to utilize their abilities at their best as they don't get benefitted from the positive interactions with family members and lack of focus in studies occurs. Counselling help can create an affectionate environment for such children to share their difficulties freely and release their mental and emotional stress. It encourages them to think of various ways to overcome the problems.

Motivation helps in achieving the goal. It is a mental as well as a psychological state which propels an organism to act for fulfilling the current need. It remains till the goal is achieved. The children who don't pay attention towards study definitely lack motivation. The students differ in their intelligence, aptitude, interest, personality, etc. These differences exist due to inherent capacities or environmental influences. Preparing the teaching learning material to cater to the individual needs of the students can yield better results. Joyful learning provides a platform to the students for their creative exposures.

The aim of education is to bring out and develop the inherent potentials & abilities of an individual. It helps in developing all aspects of an individual's personality. Guidance is the key factor in achieving these goals. We find many students lacking interest in studies. A counsellor can help in this regard by identifying the difficulties of children. He/ she can plan ways of increasing interest of children towards studies. Listening attentively, showing empathy and establishing a relationship of friendliness, mutual respect and regard help students to perform at their best.

It is human nature that he/ she wants to have the possession of things he/ she likes but in the real world, everyone has to prove his worth to get whatever he desires. Thus, self understanding and appraisal of oneself become very important in the development of realistic educational and career planning. Understanding one's own intelligence and aptitude is very important in this regard.

As we know, the whole concept of counselling is based on the understanding of human behaviour. It is quite obvious that first of all it is necessary to observe the physical, mental, and emotional set up of the children and on the basis of these observations further steps should be determined. The existence of counselling lies in solving the problems such as- stress, tensions and depression and empower people to re- incarnate themselves so that they may be able to achieve maximum as per their potentials in life.

Life is a chain of happiness and sorrow. In the midst of the moment of enjoyment, all of sudden the wheel of fortune diverts and the concerned person finds himself drowning in the ocean of despair. This is the most crucial time when counselling help is desperately needed to enable him to overcome the crisis and bring him back on the right track again. The role of counselling is essential in releasing the trauma of the sufferer. I am mentioning here a case study which reflects the importance of counselling for the needy.

It is a case of a fifteen years old boy of class IX. He suddenly became the most controversial topic in the school because a drastic change reflected in his behaviour. A shy and disciplined boy began to show aggression and intolerant behaviour with classmates as well as with some teachers. Teachers were surprised because he was getting their affection and sympathy more than usual since the sudden demise of his parents some months ago. His guardian was informed but he did not turn up. In this process, his friends disclosed that after the death of his parents, his elder sister and her husband were staying with him as a guardian. His brother- in- law was unemployed and was indulged in drinking and often created such terrible and disgusting situations at home which were tough to digest. Since the boy was unable to control whatever was going on at home, he used to show aggression to hide his fear and nervousness.

He was physically not strong enough to overpower his brother- in- law. His frustration went on increasing with each passing day. The trauma he was facing, slowly and slowly was becoming intolerable. As he was very familiar to me so I facilitated him in this regard and it took months to bring him to his normal behaviour. Actually, his problems were related to mental and emotional disorder and it required proper counselling assistance. Counselling provides a ray of hope to the depressed person who is in search of help and he shares very personal and sensitive information with the counsellor and feels relief. It provides an opportunity for releasing disturbing emotions in the presence of the counselor.

There is a myth that counselling assistance is for those only who are facing problems and are unable to bear and solve it on their own. It is true but counselling assistance is also for maximizing human growth and potential. A trained counselor provides the required help and guidance to facilitate overall development of an individual's personality. We have to pass through the choices and challenges at every stage of our life and counselling helps us to overcome the problems which come in the way.

This question is often asked- what are the main factors behind the success and failure of an individual? Sometimes, we find that a person is unable to get success despite putting valiant efforts while others taste the success easily. It is because skills, abilities, interests and aptitudes vary from person to person and knowing oneself in all aspects as well as analyzing one's own strength and weakness is very essential for achieving success. Understanding of potential and aptitude is very important while choosing a particular career.

Human development is a composite of many areas of development of an individual such as physical, cognitive, social, emotional, vocational and moral dimensions. When a person wants to choose a career, he goes through a process of decision- making. A number of personal- social and educational- vocational factors contribute to career choice making.

As we see in our family, society and profession, a majority of people are not satisfied with their careers in spite of healthy earnings because they have entered here by chance and their dreams are still chasing them to come alive. We often come across the news of suicide and violence which are becoming a part of day to day life. These are happening frequently as people are unable to cope with the stress and they become prone to surrender.

With the increasing complexities of life, stress, tensions and worries are rising rapidly and no one can escape totally from its clutches. So, counselling assistance is needed to overcome these problems and to reduce stress. Cut- throat competition, financial insecurity and job mobilization are leading towards stress. Moral values are disappearing. People are willing to acquire fame, money and power and in this regard the pressure is surmounting.

As we know that individual difference is a proven reality and everyone accepts it. Intelligence and potential of human beings cannot be at the same level but it creates a lot of problems when the differences are so much and it is termed as intellectually disabled. It is used to describe people whose Intelligence Quotient is below the normal. Sometimes our society shows very rude behaviour to them and doesn't allow them to mix up with normal people and they feel isolated which hampers their development. The people with limited intelligence not only require love and affection but also assistance from family, society and expect to meet their physical, mental and emotional needs.

Such people are part of our family and society, so it is our moral obligation to support them and try to mix them up with the mainstream. These children are slow in learning but by applying the right kind of educational techniques, it is possible. They would be able to learn basic skills of reading, writing with an extra effort on the part of the teachers. It is very important to understand that these people are not like others in learning so immense patience is needed to help them. Special educators, teachers and counselors can bring a change by providing help to the concerned person and adequate parental counselling in the initial stages would be very useful.

The parents of the children with intellectual disability face a multitude of challenges. They are not quite aware of the special needs of such children. Social isolation is also a key factor. They feel inferiority while mentioning such children. They think their social prestige may be at stake. In fact, the people are not easily ready to mix up with such people as they find it difficult to accept their abnormal behaviour. Actually, they are not educated about the individuals with intellectual disability. An orientation is required to make them aware about it.

In the present scenario, children and youth are living in tremendous pressure. They can handle the pressure of achieving their desired goals as it is related to their ambition of proving their abilities and achieving milestones. But, the pressure forced by others, especially parents, is difficult to handle. The parents are not in a position to assess the aptitude of their wards but still they pressurize their wards by forcing them to select a particular stream and jobs. They are trying to fulfil their own dreams through their wards.

As it has been proved again and again that each individual is unique in his/ her own way. The job of parents and teachers is to create suitable environments to flourish them and utilize their potentials at its best. Believing in oneself is very necessary. A person is the best judge of himself/ herself. He/ she is quite aware of his/ her strengths and weaknesses. Self- assessment provides a clear vision of one's own ability. Each individual is quite capable of performing extraordinary works as per his/ her aptitude and interests.

It is true that you can never be content and happy if you are constantly looking at others achievements who have achieved more than you. Trying to catch up with them is not a bad idea in general but other factors should also be kept in mind. Happiness and satisfaction comes from within you. It is your way of thinking which directs your happiness. When you are satisfied with whatever you have achieved, it gives you immense pleasure. Making a realistic goal helps a lot in this regard as it shows right directions and removes hindrances. Without proper planning, no one can go ahead.

When you assess yourself then you become aware of your ability and it increases self confidence and will power. The problems occur when people are not sure about themselves and are not ready to face the challenges. When you are dedicated and doing your best then it may take time in getting desired success in some cases but surety of success is always there.

Whenever you start doubting your ability, your performance will start decreasing. You should never raise doubt in yourself because your belief is the key for achieving success. Situations might be critical but they can be sorted out by you. Problems don't come to destroy you. They appear to test your ability so take these problems as routine incidents of life.

With your belief in yourself, you can change the negative aspects of life into positive one. In our life, sometimes we have to be victims of forced situations which we are unable to avoid and unwillingly become part of. It scares us if we always think about it. Particularly children and youths are very sensitive. They take such negative things very personally and it haunts them. They need emotional support to face it. Our role is to make them realize that each one has to face such happenings and these are learning lessons to achieve success in future.

We all are the creation of God. We are born on this planet to fulfill some purpose. Underestimating oneself means that we are not content with ourselves. God has given enormous power and abilities to all human beings. It can be easily justified when we look at our surroundings and find that some outstanding activities are performed by the people who were considered worthless. It suggests that we should be happy and satisfied at our position and keep on moving forward towards our goal. There is no place for regret in life whatever you couldn't achieve. Your personal achievements do matter but our precious contribution for society and nation to enrich it, matter much more.

World is full of unique and wonderful gifts of God which He has presented to us to make our life beautiful and meaningful with his blessings and our utmost efforts. So, believe in yourself and let your life blossom in your own way. Hope, you will do.

FEAR CAN BE OVERCOME– A CHALLENGE THAT LIFE ACCEPTS

We all are quite familiar that life is not as simple as we wish and throughout our life, we are destined to face numerous challenges, problems and setbacks. The differences among people who succeed in life and those who don't acquire success is due to their ability to face the challenges of life which are thrown at them at crucial juncture of their life to test their potentials and capabilities. Those who overcome the hurdles are called winners and those who are unable to cross the hurdles are termed as failures. But, life is a continuous process which consists of multi- dimensional aspects. It always provides a chance to prove his/ her worth again and again. So, instead of wandering in the realm of fear and failure, get out of yourself as quickly as possible and empower yourself to overcome all the hurdles. It is a proven reality that it is you who can make a difference.

I am quite sure that fear of failure is the biggest reason behind the people who are unable to perform at their best as per their potential and ability. It is human behaviour which prompts us to see the outcome of any given situation in both ways- positive and negative. The world is full of uncertainties. Anything can happen anytime which can change the course of life. Sometimes it may be in favour and sometimes against us. But, in any case, we are unable to control the game of destiny. In this perspective, it can be easily understood why a majority of people are inclined to take the safest way. Actually, when people think about the outcome before taking initiative of their actions, a lot of confusion occurs. The pressure keeps on mounting when they think about failure.

Generally, people underestimate their potential and ability to recover from failure. They just keep on thinking about their potential and are uncertain and thus, they miss various opportunities which could be a milestone for them. It has been proved that the ability to fail big and find often has been a mark of extraordinary success throughout history. Fear of failure is closely related to the fear of social rejection. The fear of handling pressure which comes from all the corners of the society increases stress and the concerned people are caught in a dilemma. In such a situation, some people overcome their fear of failure as they take it as a part of life process, learn from their mistakes and are determined enough to conquer it. Some people don't analyze the factors, just look at their mistakes and take it as permanent and personal and lose their self confidence.

Social imbalance is the biggest blunder on the part of society as well as nation. It is the main cause of fear of failure. As we know that each individual is an independent creature but rarely anyone gets a chance to live on their own. Their life is measured by society in terms of achievements. Society has its own small groups of individuals which are created and categorised on the basis of personal achievements. These are recognized as superiors and inferiors. No one is willing to decrease his/ her position and want to remain in the socially reputed groups. The people who are ignored always wish to reach there. The fear of being isolated from their prestigious group is always there. It has been flourishing with time.

It is high time that social imbalance needs to be solved urgently. We can't ignore any individual in our society as he is a key member and his role is equally important as others. It is very important to understand that our actions are interrelated with other members of society. If anyone's action will be ignored then it will hamper the growth of society and nation. All the people are not quite capable of doing the same work and performing at the same level and with the same pace but they are a vital cog of our society and no one can question their ability. In this regard, it is necessary to add each individual to the mainstream to make them feel as an important part of the system. When an individual will be accepted by society with unconditional love and acceptance, he will be ready and eager to give his/ her contribution at the maximum and fear of failure will disappear.

I often find that some people have a tendency of judging others instantly by their appearances, dresses, race, education, social status and their belongings. They are not authorized by anyone to do so but they are doing it due to their instinct of judging. They are judging others but in the process they forget that they are being watched and judged by others also. The question is- why do people judge others? It is a general tendency which is developing fast in society which shows people's curiosity to peep in others' lives. They are quite focused on their useless self stipulated responsibilities. They want to inspect others' actions and like to remark freely.

The people even remark about the person whom they have never seen and have never negotiated with them. It looks very strange but it can be seen everywhere in society. One of the most significant things in this process is that they categorize others with full authority as successful and failure. Even they themselves are not aware of what is the meaning of true success and failure in each individual's life. As we know, priorities of life vary from person to person. People want to achieve whatever they consider important for them. One's mission can be completely different from others. Sometimes we find that the person about whom others' perception is not positive, he, himself is busy in enjoying life as he/ she is very happy at his present situation. The people who have developed a habit of ensuring the merits and demerits of others, don't even know that their opinions don't matter for the concerned person and they are just wasting their time.

I find it strange when people make claims about a particular person that they are quite familiar with about his/ her potential and ability to handle the situation. How is it possible? We can just assume about anyone's potential but the reality can be totally different or it may be partially true or sometimes it can match with our prediction. It is my own experience that in spite of spending many years with the people, we can't predict them exactly. We can only guess on the basis of their past performance and our experience. It is often seen in society that there are numerous people who are now enjoying respected positions in society who were once discarded by society as people predicted them as a failure. These people succeeded as they were quite sure about their potentials and took the desired position through their hard work.

The truth is that no one has the ability to know you better than you, yourself. You are the witness of your feelings, emotions which are flowing inside you. You have your own unique way of seeing the world and coping with pressure. It is often said that happiness and grief reflect on an individual's face which is easily visible. It is rightly said that it doesn't matter how many times we fall but it does matter whether we are trying to get up again and again or not. There are many occasions in our lives when one is forced to hide his/ her sadness and tears to bring a smile on others face. Actually people cannot know what is going on inside you. So, sometimes when they say that you are doing great, it's the time when you are really going through adversities of life and sometimes when you are really doing great, they don't assume. That's the irony of life which we should accept without any regret.

This is the story of most of the families and societies that a majority of people are indulged in building pressure on others. Any activity or action which provides help to any individual to come out of his/ her trauma or depression is praiseworthy but few people make fun of such people. It should be immediately stopped. Social reward can be an inspiration and motivation for children. If anyone is not able to perform well and is still well supported by family and society then there are more chances to improve. He/ she will surely want to give his/ her best when he will realize that others are having faith in his ability. The problem starts when someone is neglected by family and society on the basis of one or two efforts. It is high time to realize that keeping in mind the notion of individual differences, the children should be given enough time to prove their worth.

It is necessary to understand that only hard work and determination are not sufficient for achieving desired success. Our destiny also plays a major role so when things are not going in our favour and people are criticizing and raising doubt, it is better to regroup ourselves and restore our energy to face the problems. As we know that sometimes fate like a sandstorm keeps following us in our life. We try to change our direction to escape from it but it chases us. We try again and again to negotiate but our efforts go in vain as it keeps following us everywhere and we don't find the way to come out of its reign.

The questions arise in our mind- why are we so helpless against the storm? Why are we not able to escape from it despite doing our best? Where is the source of the storm? In our search of finding the solutions, we realize that this storm is not something that blew in from far away, something that has nothing to do with us. This storm is present within us. We cannot control it at once when it comes out. What we can do is to step right inside the storm, closing our eyes and plugging our ears so that the sand does not get in and walk through it, step by step. Actually, we cannot run away from our ill- fate. As much as we try to run fast, the intensity of fear will increase so it is better to face the problem and utilize the resources and energy we have to solve the problem.

When the storm has passed, you will be amazed to see how successfully you managed to survive. At the first glance, you wouldn't believe it but it will provide you immense pleasure and satisfaction. You will still want to verify that whatever has been passed is a reality. But one thing is far sure that it will enhance your confidence to face the problem. Your self- belief will change your whole perception to see things in a broader perspective. It will be a learning lesson for your entire life and whenever such situations will again knock at your door, you will be better equipped to face them. Fear reduces our capacity to cope with the situation. It attacks people's mind like a fog and people are caught disoriented and hence are unable to find out the way.

The problem arises when people search for perfection. Everybody can be perfect in his/ her own way but nobody is perfect as a whole. When people search for perfection, it is generally related to their actions. The extraordinary performances of people from time to time categorize them as a perfect one but we are witnessing that records are breaking day by day as no one can limit and judge the potential of an individual. The expectation from others keeping in view their ability and potential is a routine process of life which we see in family, school, society, etc. Generally, it does not harm everyone but it creates pressure on the person who is in the centre of expectation. The pressure of delivering goods always follows him/ her. If he is able to sustain pressure then it is good but in the case of thinking so much on delivering good and feeling continuous stress makes it very harmful.

Why do people expect so much from others? The world of competition is full of stress. Limited number of opportunities are the biggest factor behind it. No one is quite sure about the outcome. There is always doubt. In this scenario, it is very important to understand that always try to do your best. It doesn't matter that you could not get success in one chance but it does matter that you are confident to do it and have faith in your ability. It does not make any sense if people are disappointed at your performance but it makes sense if you raise doubt on your performance. Don't allow fear of failure to enter inside you. Just keep believing in yourself and focus on your goal.

Nowadays, we can see the poverty of vision among people. As we know that it is our moral responsibility to nurture the children in a holistic way so that they can blossom in a healthy environment and would be able to show and justify their enormous potentials as per their interests and aptitudes. But, whatever is happening, is really painful. The role of parents and teachers is to support, guide and facilitate the children to perform at their level best. But, the parents are over ambitious in supporting their wards. They are not supporting them to bring out their best but they are imposing their own bundle of ambition on them and thus ignoring the interests and aptitudes of their wards.

It starts with secondary class. Children are forced to work hard to score higher marks to get Science stream in senior secondary class. After fulfilling the dream of their parents and scoring high marks, they are expected to crack IIT and medical entrance exams and the list is endless. I don't mean to say that it is the case with all the parents and their wards but it is the case with the majority of the population. The willingness of the children is generally not asked by their respective parents. Parents take the decision and their wards have to accept it. Very few children are fortunate in this regard because their parents want to know their interests and support them.

I have witnessed some instances when parents forcefully admitted their wards as per their own choices and their wards were compelled to accept it. Can you imagine the outcome? Such students are not comfortable with what was forced to accept and hence, they are unable to get desired success due to lack of interest and motivation in that specific field as it was not their personal choice. In such a situation, who is to be blamed? Parents are trying effortlessly as they want to establish their wards in the world of work so they are helping them with whatever they think is good for their wards. Their wards are not giving the outcome as per the wishes of their parents because their aptitudes do not suit the course to which they are unwillingly enrolled.

Imagine a society in which there are only doctors, engineers and administrative officers. Can you think how it will function? Life is not all about doctors, engineers, administrative officers or leaders. It requires the collective efforts from all sections of society and of each individual. We often see in the family, school and society that there is lack of transparency. Partiality is everywhere. The children who are performing well are getting support from all corners and the children who really need help to uplift themselves are generally ignored due to poor performance. In life, situations are temporary, it changes at each vital stage of life.

God has given us the ability to overpower the critical phases of life. Everyone tries to overcome fear of failure in his own way sooner or later. As we all know that fear of failure sometimes becomes very disastrous for the concerned person so it should be our moral obligation to protect our own wards and other children. In this regard, it is vital to understand that each child should be given respect in spite of his/ her performance. It is the duty of both teachers and parents to support the children and try to know their interests. There are numerous instances in history in which the people who were once rejected and humiliated in schools or by parents have proved their ability in such a way that it has become a milestone for others to achieve. Now, these are a source of inspiration for the coming generations.

The pressure of family and society affects the performance of the children. Sometimes this pressure is more on parents than their wards. They are emotionally attached so much that the success and failure of their wards hurt them continuously and they find it very difficult to cope . It has been seen that when someone develops passion to achieve something, he/ she always dreams of fulfilling it. As nothing is for granted in this world so when he/ she is unable to achieve his/ her desired success, he is prone to break down easily. Parents should understand that constant pressure can be very harmful for their wards as it will hamper their performance so instead of putting pressure on them, try to help them in adapting to the situations.

Adapting as per situation is necessary for individuals. It can be seen that some people adapt well, displaying confidence and will power in bringing desired change. Some people are unable to adapt to the situations and thus, it results in anger, frustration and depression. Adaptation defines positive thinking and response of an individual which helps him in overcoming the problems and stresses of life and he/ she feels comfortable in any given situation. We often find it in our family, neighbourhood and society that people react differently in the same situation. As we know that success and failure are part and parcel of our life and do occur. So, no need to create panic. There are many people who never lose courage and confidence. I don't mean that they feel happy at their failure, I mean that they try to analyze their mistakes and prepare better strategies next time and become more determined to achieve their goals.

It is true that whenever we don't get expected results, we get upset and become isolated. It is a momentary feeling which affects everybody but it can be sorted out through adaptive behaviour. We have seen that some people come out of a reign of disappointment within a short span of time and try to figure out where they went wrong. They try to work harder and put more commitment for their upcoming exams and they start feeling much better. These people present an example of adaptation where they have tried to deal with an unpleasant situation in a way which helped them in coming out of the crisis. Adaptation helps in dealing with one's negative feelings- sadness, frustrations and disappointments, etc. in a way which does not hamper one's functioning for an unnecessarily long period. People try to understand the reasons which prevent them from fulfilling their expectations and bring required changes in their thoughts and actions.

These types of positive and constructive ways of thinking develop confidence in our capabilities to deal with problems and challenges in our life. It facilitates us to manage stress and enables us to maintain our cool and composure irrespective of the circumstances. Actually, people tend to focus so much on the outcome before executing their plans and sometimes it paves the way for doubts. These are the impulses which create stress and anxiety and thus getting solutions to our problems becomes more difficult. It lowers our confidence in ourselves which leads to negative emotions and slows down our efficiency in dealing with everyday life situations.

Some strategies can enhance our adaptive capacity to overcome fear of failure. It is often seen that almost everyone does a lot of planning and homework regarding their actions but there are only a handful who successfully execute their plans. It happens because some people only make plans and never take initiative to start it as they are not sure about the success of their actions. They frequently raise doubts which might come true and might not come true but one thing for sure it stops them from starting their actions. On the other hand, some people make plans and start it with great enthusiasm but while approaching the way, when they have to face the problems which are bound to come, they become nervous and leave in the middle after wasting their time, money and energy.

It is quite necessary to understand that only starting is not enough. From starting onwards to achieve the desired goal, one has to complete a long way and in this process problematic situations are definite to arrive. Physical and mental alertness to face the problem helps to boost up morale in the demanding situations. Everyone has to taste the success and failure in his/ her life. If failure comes early in your life, don't feel bad, always remember that it is your turn today and it will move to the next one gradually.

Sometimes, it has been found that in spite of doing your best, you are still waiting in the wings. There is a unique method of preparing for getting success at a higher level so in such situations try to analyze the approach you have followed earlier and make required changes as per the need. Never curse yourself or destiny and don't try to make it responsible for failure. If you are doing so, it is injustice done by you for yourself. We all know that continuous efforts will never go waste so never lose hope. Always think that you are quite capable of reaching the point of success where you have dreamed to reach.

As we know that life is a learning process so each

experience of life, be it sweet or sour, is a learning lesson for the future and it helps us in avoiding the mistakes of the past. We learn from our mistakes, amend them and achieve our desired results. There are a lot of opportunities available in the world which are awaiting to be filled. Analyze your strength and weakness and then on the basis of your ability and potential, make a dedicated effort to grab it. Leave out dejection and disappointment. Try to regroup your physical, mental, emotional and spiritual energy and convert these into positive actions to get out of fear of failure and achieve your goal.

Have patience towards all that is unsolved in your heart and try to leave the questions. You will find that you are unfolding the answer one by one even without seeking the answers. You are enjoying each moment as the stress is reducing rapidly and you are feeling a lot better than before. The complications of life are disappearing and providing a sense of divine blessings. Now, the world is appearing more beautiful with your changed perception. So, stay in these feelings.

Enlighten your hope, have faith in your ability to empower yourself, accept the challenges which life has thrown at you. Believe me- fear can be overcome.

" Accept life as it is. Appreciate whatever you are endowed with. "

Raghavendra Pati Tripathi
Parul Tripathi

9 789354 729539

Printed by Libri Plureos GmbH in Hamburg,
Germany